CONTENTS

FEDERAL HEALTH PROGRAMS AND THOSE WHO CANNOT CARE FOR THEMSELVES: WHAT ARE THEIR RIGHTS AND OUR RESPONSIBILITIES?

HEARING

BEFORE THE

SUBCOMMITTEE ON CRIMINAL JUSTICE, DRUG POLICY, AND HUMAN RESOURCES

OF THE

COMMITTEE ON GOVERNMENT REFORM

HOUSE OF REPRESENTATIVES

ONE HUNDRED NINTH CONGRESS

FIRST SESSION

APRIL 19, 2005

Serial No. 109–68

Printed for the use of the Committee on Government Reform

Available via the World Wide Web: http://www.gpoaccess.gov/congress/index.html
http://www.house.gov/reform

U.S. GOVERNMENT PRINTING OFFICE

23–407 PDF WASHINGTON : 2005

For sale by the Superintendent of Documents, U.S. Government Printing Office
Internet: bookstore.gpo.gov Phone: toll free (866) 512–1800; DC area (202) 512–1800
Fax: (202) 512–2250 Mail: Stop SSOP, Washington, DC 20402–0001

COMMITTEE ON GOVERNMENT REFORM

TOM DAVIS, Virginia, *Chairman*

CHRISTOPHER SHAYS, Connecticut
DAN BURTON, Indiana
ILEANA ROS-LEHTINEN, Florida
JOHN M. McHUGH, New York
JOHN L. MICA, Florida
GIL GUTKNECHT, Minnesota
MARK E. SOUDER, Indiana
STEVEN C. LATOURETTE, Ohio
TODD RUSSELL PLATTS, Pennsylvania
CHRIS CANNON, Utah
JOHN J. DUNCAN, JR., Tennessee
CANDICE S. MILLER, Michigan
MICHAEL R. TURNER, Ohio
DARRELL E. ISSA, California
GINNY BROWN-WAITE, Florida
JON C. PORTER, Nevada
KENNY MARCHANT, Texas
LYNN A. WESTMORELAND, Georgia
PATRICK T. McHENRY, North Carolina
CHARLES W. DENT, Pennsylvania
VIRGINIA FOXX, North Carolina
——— ———

HENRY A. WAXMAN, California
TOM LANTOS, California
MAJOR R. OWENS, New York
EDOLPHUS TOWNS, New York
PAUL E. KANJORSKI, Pennsylvania
CAROLYN B. MALONEY, New York
ELIJAH E. CUMMINGS, Maryland
DENNIS J. KUCINICH, Ohio
DANNY K. DAVIS, Illinois
WM. LACY CLAY, Missouri
DIANE E. WATSON, California
STEPHEN F. LYNCH, Massachusetts
CHRIS VAN HOLLEN, Maryland
LINDA T. SANCHEZ, California
C.A. DUTCH RUPPERSBERGER, Maryland
BRIAN HIGGINS, New York
ELEANOR HOLMES NORTON, District of Columbia
———
BERNARD SANDERS, Vermont (Independent)

MELISSA WOJCIAK, *Staff Director*
DAVID MARIN, *Deputy Staff Director/Communications Director*
ROB BORDEN, *Parliamentarian/Senior Counsel*
TERESA AUSTIN, *Chief Clerk*
PHIL BARNETT, *Minority Chief of Staff/Chief Counsel*

SUBCOMMITTEE ON CRIMINAL JUSTICE, DRUG POLICY, AND HUMAN RESOURCES

MARK E. SOUDER, Indiana, *Chairman*

PATRICK T. McHENRY, North Carolina
DAN BURTON, Indiana
JOHN L. MICA, Florida
GIL GUTKNECHT, Minnesota
STEVEN C. LATOURETTE, Ohio
CHRIS CANNON, Utah
CANDICE S. MILLER, Michigan
GINNY BROWN-WAITE, Florida
VIRGINIA FOXX, North Carolina

ELIJAH E. CUMMINGS, Maryland
BERNARD SANDERS, Vermont
DANNY K. DAVIS, Illinois
DIANE E. WATSON, California
LINDA T. SANCHEZ, California
C.A. DUTCH RUPPERSBERGER, Maryland
MAJOR R. OWENS, New York
ELEANOR HOLMES NORTON, District of Columbia

EX OFFICIO

TOM DAVIS, Virginia
HENRY A. WAXMAN, California

J. MARC WHEAT, *Staff Director*
MICHELLE GRESS, *Counsel*
MALIA HOLST, *Clerk*
TONY HAYWOOD, *Minority Counsel*

FEDERAL HEALTH PROGRAMS AND THOSE WHO CANNOT CARE FOR THEMSELVES: WHAT ARE THEIR RIGHTS AND OUR RESPONSIBILITIES?

TUESDAY, APRIL 19, 2005

HOUSE OF REPRESENTATIVES,
SUBCOMMITTEE ON CRIMINAL JUSTICE, DRUG POLICY, AND HUMAN RESOURCES,
COMMITTEE ON GOVERNMENT REFORM,
Washington, DC.

The subcommittee met, pursuant to notice, at 2 p.m., in room 2154, Rayburn House Office Building, Hon. Mark Souder (chairman of the committee) presiding.

Present: Represenatives Souder, Cummings, McHenry, Norton, Brown-Waite, and Watson.

Staff present: J. Marc Wheat, staff director and chief counsel; Michelle Gress, Counsel; David Thommason and Pat Dequattro, congressional fellows; Melia Holst, clerk; Tony Haywood, minority counsel; and Jean Gosa, minority assistant clerk.

Mr. SOUDER. The subcommittee will now come to order.

Good afternoon and thank you all for being here for this important hearing. A special thank you to our witnesses, some of whom have traveled a great distance and all of whom are going to give us the benefit of their knowledge and experience today.

The hearing today is "Federal Health Programs and Those Who Cannot Care for Themselves: What are Their Rights and Our Responsibilities?" We hope to examine the report provided by the Federal Medicaid and Medicare programs for the ordinary care of incapacitated citizens who are not in the dying process. The people we are talking about as incapacitated citizens cannot speak for themselves and cannot care for themselves. They necessarily require long term care of family, community or institutions to live.

Although there are provisions within Medicare and Medicaid that address advanced medical directives of such individuals, the provisions do not address many issues surrounding the ordinary care of incapacitated individuals.

These are issues that have been raised in light of the tragic Terri Schiavo situation and which now deserve our focused attention and exploration. First among these issues is whether, in the absence of some sort of advanced medical directive or express medical power of attorney, there should be a Federal presumption in favor of life so that a Medicare or Medicaid patient who is incapacitated is not denied ordinary care such as hydration and nutrition without due process and full exercise of their rights as human beings to fight their incapacity.

This is our point of departure and although we may leave here with more questions than answers today, it is important to examine what types of treatment options are available for incapacitated citizens who are not in the dying process, whether the various legal instruments such as advanced medical directives or medical powers of attorney are sufficient and what protections exist for incapacitated individuals to ensure that their Constitutional rights of due process are met.

At a minimum, our Federal programs should protect patients rather than pave the way to hasten their death but we do not have a Federal presumption where a person's wishes are unknown and unknowable. This creates a vacuum where someone else may determine that a patient's life is not one worth living and this is most definitely a slippery slope.

Let me quote at length a homily given by Archbishop Galen which underlines the importance of staying vigilant against new developments in the law that run counter to a Judeo-Christian understanding of human dignity. "If you establish and apply the principle that you can kill unproductive human beings then woe betide to all of us who become old and frail. If one is allowed to kill unproductive people, then woe betide the invalids who have been used up, sacrificed or lost their health and strength in the productive process. Poor people, sick people, unproductive people, so what? Have they somehow forfeited the right to live? Do you, do I have the right to live only as long as we are productive? Nobody would be safe anymore. Who could trust his physician? It is inconceivable what deprived conduct, what suspicion would enter family life if this terrible doctrine is tolerated, adopted and carried out."

Archbishop Clemmons Von Galen was not speaking out as a consequence of the Terri Schiavo controversy. He anticipated it. Archbishop Clemmons Von Galen spoke these words from the pulpit on August 3, 1941 against a euthanasia program being instituted by the German government. The sermon was aimed at a specific policy and a specific time and place but he touched upon a recurrent theme that transcends place and time. It is a helpful warning from history to guide our footsteps on our uncertain post-Schiavo path.

We have a variety of witnesses joining us today to help us with some of these important issues. Our first panel consists of Representative Dave Weldon of the 15th district of Florida. Congressman Weldon is an esteemed former member of the Government Reform Committee and former chairman of the Census Subcommittee of this committee. Congressman Weldon is also a medical doctor and brings his unique perspective and experience on Federal health care matters to this hearing today.

Our second panel consists of Dr. Donald Young, Deputy Assistant Secretary for Planning and Evaluation, Department of Health and Human Services who in his medical practice has firsthand experience with end of life care.

Our third and final panel consists of four witnesses: Diane Coleman, president and founder of a disability advocacy rights group called Not Dead Yet; Bob Sedlmeyer from my congressional district in Indiana. Bob has a 19-year-old daughter, Valerie, who has been incapacitated since birth and for whom Bob and his wife, Cheryl, provide in-home care. Kay Adamson has had a severe stroke and experienced what is known as "locked-in syndrome." Although she was conscious and aware, she was physically, totally unresponsive. At one point, her doctors withdrew all nutrition and hydration from her. Last, we have Professor Robert Destro from the Columbus School of Law at the Catholic University. He served for 6 years as a commissioner with the U.S. Commission on Civil Rights and led the Commission's discussions in the areas of discrimination on the basis of disability.

I would like to yield to our distinguished ranking member, Mr. Cummings of Maryland, for an opening statement.

[The prepared statement of Hon. Mark E. Souder follows:]

Opening Statement
Chairman Mark Souder

"Federal Health Programs and Those Who Cannot Care for Themselves: What Are Their Rights, and Our Responsibilities?"

Subcommittee on Criminal Justice, Drug Policy, and Human Resources
Committee on Government Reform

April 19, 2005

Good afternoon and thank you all for being here for this important hearing. A special thank you to our witnesses, as well, some of whom have traveled a great distance and all of whom are giving us the benefit of their knowledge and experience today.

The hearing today is "Federal Health Programs and Those Who Cannot Care for Themselves: What are Their Rights and Our Responsibilities." We hope to examine the support provided by federal Medicaid and Medicare programs for ordinary care of incapacitated citizens who are not in the dying process.

The people we are talking about, as incapacitated citizens, cannot speak for themselves, and cannot care for themselves. They necessarily require the long term care of family, community or institutions to live. Although there are provisions within Medicaid and Medicare that address advance medical directives of such individuals, the provisions do not address many issues surrounding the ordinary care of incapacitated individuals.

These are issues that have been raised in light of the tragic Terri Schiavo situation, and which now deserve our focused attention and exploration.

First among these issues is whether, in the absence some sort of advance medical directive or express medical power of attorney, there should be a *federal presumption in favor of life*, so that a Medicare or Medicaid patient who is incapacitated is not denied ordinary care such as hydration or nutrition without due process, and full exercise of their rights as human beings, despite their incapacity.

This is our point of departure, and although we may leave here with more questions than answers today, it's important to examine what types of treatment options are available for incapacitated citizens who are not in the dying process; whether the various legal instruments – such as advance medical directives or medical powers of attorney – are sufficient; and what protections exist for incapacitated individuals to ensure that their constitutional rights of due process are met.

At a minimum, our federal programs should protect patients rather than pave the way to hasten their death, but we do not have a federal presumption where a person's wishes are unknown and unknowable. This creates a vacuum where someone else may determine that a patient's life is one not worth living, and this is most definitely a slippery slope. Let me quote at length a homily given by Archbishop Galen, which underlines the importance of staying vigilant against new developments in the law that run counter to a Judeo-Christian understanding of human dignity:

> *If you establish and apply the principle that you can 'kill' unproductive human beings, then woe betide us all when we become old and frail! If one is allowed to kill unproductive people, then woe betide the invalids who have used up, sacrificed and lost their health and strength in the productive process... Poor people, sick people, unproductive people, so what? Have they somehow forfeited the right to live? Do you, do I, have the right to live only as long as we are productive?... Nobody would be safe anymore. Who could trust his physician? It is inconceivable what depraved conduct, what suspicion would enter family life if this terrible doctrine is tolerated, adopted, carried out.*

Archbishop Clemens von Galen was not speaking out as a consequence of the Terri Schiavo controversy – he anticipated it. Archbishop Clemens von Galen spoke these words from the pulpit on August 3, 1941 against a euthanasia program being instituted by the German government. The sermon was aimed at a specific policy in a specific place and time, but he touched upon a recurrent theme that transcends place and time. It is a helpful warning from history, to guide our footsteps on our uncertain, post-Schiavo, path.

We have a variety of witnesses joining us today to help draw out some of these important issues. Our first panel consists of Representative Dave Weldon, of the 15th district of Florida. Congressman Weldon is an esteemed former member of the Government Reform committee, and former Chairman of the Census Subcommittee. Congressman Weldon is also a medical doctor, and brings his unique perspective and experience on federal health care matters to this hearing today.

Our second panel consists of Dr. Donald A. Young, the Deputy Assistant Secretary for Planning and Evaluation at Health and Human Services, who in his medical practice has first hand experience with end of life care.

Our third and final panel consists of four witnesses: Diane Coleman, President and Founder of a disability rights advocacy group called Not Dead Yet.

Bob Sedlmeyer, from my Congressional district in Indiana. Bob has a nineteen year-old daughter, Valerie, who has been incapacitated since birth, and for whom Bob and his wife provide in-home care.

Kate Adamson, who had a severe stroke and experienced what is known as "locked-in syndrome." Although she was conscious and aware, she was physically totally unresponsive, and at one point her doctors withdrew all nutrition and hydration from her.

And Professor Robert Destro, from the Columbus School of Law of Catholic University. He served for six years as a commissioner on the United States Commission on Civil Rights, and led the Commission's discussions in the areas of discrimination on the basis of disability.

Mr. CUMMINGS. Thank you very much, Mr. Chairman.

One of the responsibilities I take most seriously as a legislator involves protecting the interests of the most vulnerable segments of our society. Individuals who are incapacitated by reason of illness, injury, birth defect or advanced age are among those whose rights and interests we must be most vigilant in protecting.

Decisions affecting a patient's course of medical treatment are, of course, among the most personal and consequential decisions that a person can make or that can be made on a person's behalf. When a person cannot make such decisions on his own, society must do what it can to ensure that the decision is made in the best interest of the patient's health and/or in accordance with the patient's own wishes and legal rights.

In some instances these interests can be difficult to sort out, particularly when it comes to deciding whether to provide or withhold life sustaining treatment for a severely incapacitated person who stands no realistic chance of improving.

The Supreme Court has made it clear that a person has a Constitutional right to refuse life sustaining treatment if that is what he or she wishes. In the absence of a clear advanced directive or living will document, however, determining what a patient who cannot communicate would want can give rise to an awful dilemma for the family or guardian of the patient.

We all witnessed this in the controversial case of Terri Schiavo and perhaps many of us have faced this kind of decision in our own families. Certainly there can be few decisions more grave or heart wrenching for a family to confront whether or when to give up on the life of a loved one who may be a shadow of his or her former self or for whom the medical outlook is terribly grim or bleak.

For that reason, I think the Schiavo case teaches us that the most constructive approach we can take as policymakers is to help families to avoid such dilemmas by encouraging the use of living wills and by educating members of the public about their rights to elect or to refuse life sustaining treatment should they become severely incapacitated.

According to a 2002 study funded by the Robert Wood Johnson Foundation, only 15 to 20 percent of Americans have living wills. That is why I am an original co-sponsor of legislation that will be introduced in the House by Representative Sander Levin of Michigan, the "Advanced Directives Improvement and Education Act of 2005" co-authored with Senator Bill Nelson of Florida which would ensure that a person's advanced directive is known and respected, that a person can obtain professional advice in preparation of such a directive, and that the information on State laws is broadly available to those who wish to exercise their rights.

While I supported the Schiavo bill, I think the best role for Congress to play in moving forward is to empower our citizens to make these crucial decisions with adequate planning and forethought. Moreover, Congress should give thorough and deliberate consideration to any changes we might contemplate making to the existing system.

There can be no easy or painless answer in an end of life decision scenario. We can make it easier for families to be sure that the rights and wishes of their loved ones are honored and protected when tragic circumstances give rise to so awful a predicament.

That said, Mr. Chairman, we all know there are many perspectives and many factors, both legal and moral to consider when it comes to how we formulate policy on caring for those who lack or lose the ability to care for or make decisions for themselves. We will hear some of those perspectives today and I look forward to the testimony of each of our witnesses.

With that, Mr. Chairman, I yield.

Mr. SOUDER. Thank you.

We have been joined by the vice chairman of the subcommittee, Mr. McHenry of North Carolina.

Mr. MCHENRY. Thank you.

I would like to first thank all of our witnesses today. I look forward to hearing or reading your testimony. Thank you, Congressman Weldon, for being here as a medical expert. We certainly appreciate your leadership on this tough and important issue.

Today, we will be examining the support given by Medicaid and Medicare programs for the ordinary care of citizens who are incapacitated but are not dying. That is the key distinction we are looking at, these individuals who are not dying and whose rights must be protected. The incapacitated cannot speak for themselves but as citizens they have the same right to life as you and I, rights guaranteed by the Constitution. People who are incapacitated require long-term care provided by family, community and medical institutions in order to survive. Medicare and Medicaid do not address many of the issues surrounding the ordinary care these helpless people need to survive. This is an issue that recently came to light through the tragic death of Terry Schiavo. We need to fill in the gaps in the current Medicare and Medicaid system so that in the future no one else must suffer like Ms. Schiavo and the Schindler family.

First among these issues is whether there should be a Federal presumption in favor of life in the absence of an advanced medical directive or express medical power of attorney. This was the crux of the situation involving Ms. Schiavo, an individual who was incapacitated, but in many medical opinions, was not dying and where there was medical uncertainty as to her wishes due to the lack of an advance medical directive or power of medical attorney. A presumption in favor of life would ensure that a Medicare or Medicaid patient who was incapacitated like Ms. Schiavo, is not denied ordinary care such as hydration or nutrition without the due process that is guaranteed all citizens including those on death row.

This is a very complicated issue, made more difficult by the fact that State laws are inconsistent and there is currently no Federal provision to resolve these conflicts. However, we must work through these areas of confusion to examine three things: first, the various treatment options available to incapacitated citizens who are not dying; second, if the legal instruments meant to protect them are sufficient; and three, whether there are enough legal protections to ensure that the Constitutional right to due process of capacitated individuals is met.

Currently, there is no Federal presumption when a person's wishes are unknown. I believe that in such situations where there is a legitimate due process question, we must always side on the side of life. Life or death is the most important question and the most important decision. As such, it must not be made for someone else when there is even the slightest possibility of doubt as to their wishes. Human life must be protected.

We are very fortunate today to have four wonderful panels that will take on these questions and many others. I look forward to hearing this discussion, Mr. Chairman.

Mr. SOUDER. Ms. Norton, do you have an opening statement?

Ms. NORTON. I am sorry I won't be here for much of this hearing, I have two other hearings going on at the same time. I am intrigued that the Criminal Justice Subcommittee would be having this hearing today. I am trying to fathom that in light of the areas in which you have traditionally concentrated.

I certainly don't have any objection to the hearing. I think the Schiavo case raises issues that ought to be discussed in precisely this kind of setting as opposed to a setting forced upon us in the past.

I very much regret, though, that this hearing did not become the opportunity as well to correct some of the impressions that were left in the wake of the Schiavo hearings. It questions the maligning of compassionate care at the end of life by hospices by members and others repeatedly talking about people being starved to death and people being deprived of water to their death when you don't have to be a professional to understand that hospices are embraced by Americans precisely because they help people avoid a painful death. They are regulated by the States, sharply regulated. I thought they did a huge disservice to allow stand. It would have been good to have someone here to speak to that issue.

It would have been good if we were going to have this hearing to have some witness come forward to testify about living wills. Everywhere I go people virtually come up to you and say, make sure I have told you, now you know it and most of them are saying they don't want to continue to live under those circumstances but the point is, and perhaps one of the most important points driven home by the Schiavo case is the living will point. I would like to know more about that as long as we are having this hearing. I regret there is no witness who can testify as to that.

Finally, I regret that there is not some expert there who could tell us the extent to which, and it is a huge extent, of families making precisely the decision that the Schiavo family made with respect to Terri. That is to say every day of the week, feeding tubes, if you will, are given up because either a court intervenes or because the family makes that decision. No family would ever make that decision if a dying person starved to death and experienced starvation or if a dying person experienced the need for water and was denied it. When virtually the entire neurological profession said that those feelings were impossible in a woman whose brain had dissolved to the extent that her brain had dissolved, it seems to me that the kind of fairness you are known for in this hearing would have required some witnesses to come forward to speak to at least some of those issues which are also involved.

I note and I asked when I came in were there any other witnesses and they said there was a witness that could not attend and that the minority was given but I just raise these issues because I think the kind of discussion you have started here is an important one and I congratulate you for starting it. That is exactly what we need but I think we need to have all the elements brought into the discussion and they do not seem to be included in the witness list.

I have two other hearings going on, literally, important hearings and I cannot stay for this hearing but I certainly have staff here so that I can begin to understand whether some of these issues were discussed.

I thank you again, Mr. Chairman, for starting this discussion in the Congress, a vital discussion indeed.

Mr. SOUDER. Thank you and if you could briefly explain the process of how this happened. At the beginning of this session, the Department of Health and Human Services was moved to our committee. As the gentlelady knows and everybody here, we can barely cover all the other things that we are covering but we start to occasionally have hearings in the Department of HHS along with the full committee, for example, the COX2 inhibitor hearings are going to be in the full committee and occasionally those hearings will be there and occasionally in this subcommittee.

Ordinarily, this was going to be a full committee hearing. They asked to move it to the subcommittee and at my request, we have tried to have it not focused just on the Terri Schiavo case where it was originally headed and try to look at the issue from a broader perspective and hopefully not only this committee but others will look at it in many of the ways and aspects that you raise.

Congresswoman Brown-Waite, do you have an opening statement?

Ms. BROWN-WAITE. Yes, I do.

I want to thank you very much for calling this hearing on how to best protect the rights of those who cannot care for themselves, including the terminally ill and those Americans who are incapacitated but not in the dying process.

The controversy surrounding the death of Terri Schiavo hit close to home for all of us. One lesson we can take from her passing is the importance of creating a living will and completing a health care surrogate form. These forms make a person's wishes clear and ensure they are clearly documented and legally binding.

I have agreed to co-sponsor House Resolution 217 which is a bipartisan resolution encouraging all Americans to set forth their medical wishes through a living will. By drafting a living will, individuals are able to ease the burden placed on their loved ones by making serious medical decisions before they are incapacitated or unable to articulate their wishes to medical personnel.

This oversight hearing also seeks to examine the Federal role in decisions relating to long term care of incapacitated Americans that rely on Medicare and Medicaid programs. The proper role of the Federal Government in these situations presently is not clear. We must, however, be very careful that we are not usurping any family decisionmaking given the importance of this issue raised by recent events.

I thank the chairman for holding this hearing today and I look forward to our discussions and hearing from our very capable witnesses.

Thank you and I yield back the balance of my time.

Mr. SOUDER. Before proceeding, I would like to take care of a couple of procedural matters. First, I ask unanimous consent that all Members have 5 legislative days to submit written statements and questions for the hearing record and the answers to written questions provided by the witnesses also be included in the record. Without objection, so ordered.

I also ask unanimous consent that all exhibits, documents and other materials referred to by Members and the witnesses may be included in the hearing record, that all Members be permitted to revise and extend their remarks. Without objection, so ordered.

If there is a Member of the House or Senate who is testifying, they are always the first panel. It is customary to ask all our witnesses to testify under oath but as Members of Congress, we take that oath at the beginning of the year.

Our first panel is Dr. Dave Weldon.

Dr. Weldon. I would be very happy to take the oath again, Mr. Chairman, if you would like.

Mr. SOUDER. Our first panel is Dr. David Weldon, a Member of the House of Representatives. Thank you and we would welcome your opening statement at this time.

STATEMENT OF HON. DAVE WELDON, A REPRESENTATIVE IN CONGRESS FROM THE STATE OF FLORIDA

Dr. WELDON. I am delighted to be here, Chairman Souder, and Ranking Member Cummings and members of the committee. I appreciate the opportunity to testify before the subcommittee and to discuss the issues surrounding the rights of the disabled, our responsibilities to protect the disabled in end of life decisions and the nexus of Federal health programs with regard to protecting vulnerable adults.

As you know, I introduced H.R. 1151, legislation designed to give greater legal scrutiny to incapacitated individuals in situations like that of Terri Schiavo to ensure that before their life is ended by depriving of necessary fluids and nutrition, a final review be granted through the Federal courts.

I want to thank you, Mr. Chairman, as well as the ranking member and Mr. Danny Davis of the committee for co-sponsoring that legislation. In addition, I am thankful to the broad spectrum of support we received on this issue from such people as the Reverend Jesse Jackson, Ralph Nader, Nat Hentoff and many others.

This issue we are about to discuss today transcends party labels. By introducing H.R. 1151, I was attempting to address the deficiencies of a system that advocates starvation and dehydration of those who are dependent on others for their care. While many have taken from the Terri Schiavo a heightened interest in living wills, I believe it would be wise for us to broaden that discussion beyond legal documents.

I was shocked to learn in a recently released report that 80 percent of States now allow doctors and hospitals to controvert the express wishes of individuals in those legal wills and advance directives. The problem goes deeper than not having the proper forms. That same report goes on to say that "Increasingly health care providers who consider a patient's quality of life too low are denying life preserving measures against the will of patients and families and the laws of most States provide no effective protection against this involuntary denial."

I encourage this committee to look at and consider deficiencies that exist in Federal laws that set conditions for participation in the Medicare and Medicaid programs and how essential care such as food and fluids are being dispensed. Medicare considers the provision of food and fluids through a feeding tube as a prosthetic medical intervention. Yet, the enforcement of this requirement is clearly lacking.

To address this weakness, I believe it is imperative to create a substantive standard addressing when food and fluids can be withdrawn to ensure that the rights of incapacitated individuals are not violated. In my view, that standard would presume that vulnerable adults would want to be fed and given fluids unless they had expressly expressed otherwise. It is important that we err on the side of providing this type of care in the absence of an explicit written directive and that the Federal standard be expressed clearly to all health providers.

Our legal system is weighted very heavily toward ensuring that we do not convict the wrong person and we are improving upon this system every day, as an example with the addition of DNA evidence in particular. Should we not also as a society err on the side of preserving the life of an incapacitated individual? Incapacitation is not something any of us would choose but to bring about an end to that condition based on hearsay or anecdotal evidence should not be sufficient in the eyes of any court or legislative body. The lack of a standard that says we ought not starve incapacitated persons to death is in part the result of a chilling trend that substitutes utilitarian judgments of medical ethicesis for the minimal care and compassion required to simply feed someone and provide them with water.

This march toward redefining humanity and classifying the incapacitated as non-persons is a dangerous step that strips the most vulnerable of the founding principles on which this country was founded. We must be careful as a Nation not to travel down the perilous path of nations that have treated those with disabilities including those with severe brain damage as less than whole persons. History has not judged favorably those societies.

The utilitarian trend plays into the epidemic of elder abuse and neglect occurring in many long term care facilities around America. What is needed is accurate data and information about gaps in detection, investigation and intervention into the neglect and exploitation of vulnerable and incapacitated adults wherever it may occur.

With this committee's assistance, it is my desire to introduce legislation that would address the needs and deficiencies I have cited by one, establishing a clear, substantive standard regarding basic care such as food and water; two, initiate an appropriate study to clearly identify areas of neglect and abuse that our vulnerable and incapacitated adults and children face today; and three, to establish a Federal presumption in our Medicaid and Medicare programs that fluid and food will not be denied absent an explicit wish to the contrary.

Mr. Chairman, these past few weeks have shown us that what we may have considered normal, appropriate care for incapacitated individuals, namely the provision of food and fluids, is now being challenged. Congress must step up to this challenge and be prepared to affirm the full protections and rights of every American but most especially those dependent on others. Let it not be said that we ignored so important a value.

Thank you for your interest in this subject. I would be very happy to field any questions you or thc others may have.

[The prepared statement of Hon. Dave Weldon follows:]

Statement of Rep. Dave Weldon, M.D. (FL-15)
April 19, 2005

Thank you for the opportunity to testify before the Subcommittee and to discuss the issues surrounding the rights of the vulnerable, our responsibilities to protect the vulnerable in end-of-life decisions, and the nexus of federal health programs with regard to protecting vulnerable adults.

As you know, I introduced H.R. 1151, legislation designed to give greater legal scrutiny to incapacitated individuals in situations like that of Terri Schiavo, to ensure that before their life is ended by depriving them of necessary fluids and nutrition, a final review was granted through the federal courts.

I want to thank Chairman Souder, Ranking Member Cummings, and Mr. Davis for co-sponsoring that legislation. In addition, I am thankful for the broad spectrum of support we received on this issue from such people as Rev. Jesse Jackson, Ralph Nader, Nat Hentoff and others. This issue we are about to discuss today transcends party labels.

By introducing H.R. 1151, I was attempting to address the deficiencies of a system that advocates starvation and dehydration of those who are dependent on others for their care.

While many have taken from the Terri Schiavo tragedy a heightened interest in living wills, I believe it would be wise for us to broaden that discussion beyond legal documents. I was shocked to learn in a recently released report that 80 percent of states now allow doctors and hospitals to controvert the expressed wishes of individuals in those written legal wills and advanced directives.

No, the problem goes deeper than not having the proper forms. That same report goes on to say that, quote, "Increasingly, health care providers who consider a patient's "quality of life" too low are denying life-preserving measures against the will of patients and families – and the laws of most states provide no effective protection against this involuntary denial."

I encourage this committee to look at and consider deficiencies that exist in federal law setting conditions for participation in the Medicare and Medicaid programs and how essential care such as food and fluids are being dispensed. Medicare considers the provision of food and fluids through a feeding tube as a prosthetic medical intervention. Yet, the enforcement of this requirement is clearly lacking.

To address this weakness, I believe it is imperative to create a substantive standard addressing when food and fluids can be withdrawn to ensure that the rights of incapacitated individuals are not violated.

In my view, that standard would presume that vulnerable adults would want to be fed and given fluids unless they had explicitly expressed otherwise. It is important that we err on the side of providing this type of care in the absence of an explicit written directive, and that this federal standard be expressed clearly to all health providers.

Our legal system is weighted very heavily toward ensuring that we do not convict the wrong person, and we are improving upon this system every day with the addition of DNA evidence in particular.

Should we not also as a society err on the side of preserving the life of an incapacitated individual? Incapacitation is not something any of us would choose, but to bring about an end to that condition based on hearsay or anecdotal evidence should not be sufficient in the eyes of any court or legislative body.

The lack of a standard that says we ought not starve incapacitated persons to death is in part the result of a chilling trend that substitutes utilitarian judgments of medical ethicists for the minimal care and compassion required to simply feed someone and provide them with water.

This march toward re-defining humanity and classifying the incapacitated as "non-persons" is a dangerous step that strips the most vulnerable of the founding principles on which this country was founded. We must be careful as a nation, not to travel down the perilous path of nations that have treated those with disabilities, including those with severe brain damage, as less than whole persons. History has not judged favorably those societies.

This utilitarian trend plays into the epidemic of elder abuse and neglect occurring in many long-term care facilities around America. What is needed is accurate data and information about gaps in detection, investigation, and intervention into the neglect and exploitation of vulnerable and incapacitated adults wherever it may occur.

With this committee's assistance, it is my desire to introduce legislation that would address the needs and deficiencies I have cited by 1.) Establishing a clear a substantive standard regarding basic care such as food and fluids; 2.) Initiate an appropriate study to clearly identify areas of neglect and abuse that our vulnerable and incapacitated adults face today; and 3.) To establish a federal presumption in our Medicaid and Medicare programs that food and fluids will not be denied absent an explicit wish to the contrary.

Mr. Chairman, these past few weeks have shown us that what we may have considered normal, appropriate care for incapacitated individuals—namely the provision of food and fluids—is now being challenged. Congress must step up to this challenge and be prepared to affirm the full protections and rights of every American but most especially those that are dependent on others. Let it not be said that we ignored so important a value.

Mr. Chairman, thank you for your interest in this subject.

Mr. SOUDER. Let me read a statement from the U.S. Conference of Catholic Bishops and if you could react to this as a doctor, I would appreciate it. They said, “We reject any omission of nutrition and hydration intended to cause a patient's death. We hold for the presumption in favor of providing medical assisted nutrition and hydration to patients who need it which presumption would yield in cases where such procedures have no medically reasonable hope of sustaining life, propose excessive risk or burdens.” Practically speaking, as a doctor, how is a decision reached that a procedure has “no medically reasonable hope of sustaining life or pose excessive risk or burdens?” Should those considerations override Federal presumptions to support nutrition and hydration?

Dr. WELDON. That statement from the Catholic Bishops, I have seen and, it is probably one of the most thoughtful statements on this issue that I have read. These issues are very, very tricky and as I said on multiple occasions during the controversy surrounding the Terri Schiavo case, there were instances where I withdrew food and fluids. An example would be dealing with somebody who was very elderly and perhaps somewhat disabled with failing health, multiple medical problems, say they had an underlying heart or lung condition and then developed another complication and would have say a massive stroke. They would be in the hospital and we would get into these issues. It is a very fine line and requires very skilled and experienced judgment when you are crossing over the edge where you are no longer preserving life but you are now prolonging the dying process. In that circumstance, I would sometimes either not initiate food and fluids or if they had already been initiated on occasions I would stop them. Of course this was after full and detailed consultation with family members.

In that statement, the Catholic bishops have a presumption that you will give food and fluid but they go on to qualify that which presumption would yield in cases where such procedures have no medically reasonable hope of sustaining life or pose excessive risk or burden and that is the kind of circumstance I was talking about, somebody who was clearly in the process of passing away and what would otherwise be a process that might take 2 or 3 days, it can be viewed as inhumane to drag that out over weeks or months.

I don't think the Terri Schiavo case fit that description I am describing to you at all. I think it was a very, very different circumstance. Any change in Federal regulations involving the Medicare and Medicaid programs have to take these kinds of nuances into consideration. If we are going to establish a standard that food and fluids will be a requirement, it has to be caveated in such a way that it allows for professional judgment in situations where you are not prolonging life, you are actually prolonging the dying process.

As well, obviously any change in Federal laws or regulations have to take into account any advance directives that the patients may have put forward.

Mr. SOUDER. You have been involved in variations of this issue since you have been in Congress. Have you seen HHS take any intervention, set any guidelines and is your bill trying to address some of that?

Dr. WELDON. I have not personally seen any HHS directive, but I believe you have a witness from HHS coming forward. The trend I am concerned about and why I think it is appropriate for us to intervene in this situation is 10 years ago, 15 years ago, you would often have families wanting to withdraw food and fluid in what was perceived as a helpless situation and you would have health care providers who were not comfortable with that decision and wanted to continue to administer food and fluid. Some of those cases ended up in court and I believe the Karen Quinlan case fell into that category.

Now what you are actually seeing in the health care delivery system is circumstances where either you have no advance directive or you have stated directives from the patients to have food and fluid and sometimes actually written directives as the report I cited to you stated, family members who are wanting it and health care providers who are saying the quality of life here is insufficient to justify this and they are unilaterally withdrawing food and fluids over the objections of patients and family members and there is no standard in many States in law to basically contravene any of this.

Mr. SOUDER. Mr. Cummings.

Mr. CUMMINGS. As I was listening to you, I could not help but think about the many people who called my office with regard to the Schiavo case and many of them very emotional. I have never seen anything like it. These were people who felt that for the most part they should just let her pass away. The interesting thing is a lot of them had been through the experience.

I think it is so sad that this has gotten so tangled up in politics. Different people have different perspectives. I was hoping this hearing would put the politics aside, which I think we are trying to do, and try to address what you just said. Listening to what you just said, it kind of makes me understand how it could get so emotional because what you just said to me is a pretty complicated, individual kind of decision. I heard what you said, instead of prolonging life, you are prolonging death. I take it doctors can disagree or agree on that? Is that reasonable to believe? I don't know, I am asking you. Is that the standard and how do you codify that? Do you follow me?

Dr. WELDON. Absolutely. Let me share with you, politicians aren't the only people who disagree on issues and doctors frequently caring for patients will disagree on treatments and interventions. What I had seen 10 and 15 years ago was a tendency, and I think some of this grew out of concern for litigation, that a lot of doctors would just throw technology at anybody and everybody and put lots of people who shouldn't have been put on life sustaining modalities, on them and you would frequently have patient family members coming forward and saying, no, we don't want this.

The trend now seems to be actually in the opposite direction which is I think beyond the Schiavo case, for the Congress actually looking at this. People against their written directives, people against their family members' desires are having food and fluid withdrawn.

Regarding the specifics of the Schiavo case, we need to keep in mind that case, while the media I think went to great lengths to portray it as a Republican-Democrat kind of thing, it totally transcended that when you actually looked at the yeas and nays and when you looked at who signed on the original bill. Some very serious concerns were also expressed about the way that case was handled.

This issue is going to continue to be a problem in my opinion and we as a body are going to come under increasing pressure to help contain costs in the Federal health programs and as well insurers are going to come under increased pressure from policyholders, premium payers to contain costs. So when you are talking about something as fundamental as food and water, I think it is very appropriate for the Congress of the United States to explore this issue. I think a standard needs to be established and any standard we establish in the Federal programs have the high likelihood of becoming a standard in private practice as well.

Mr. CUMMINGS. When you say costs, you are not talking about the food and the water. Costs go to a person being in a bed in a facility with people looking after them. You said the reverse has now happened where the doctors may take them off the food and water.

Dr. WELDON. That is happening today in America.

Mr. CUMMINGS. I want to ask you this. Do you think a lot of that has to do with costs?

Dr. WELDON. Yes, I do. I think a lot of the physicians in the institutions look at the cost of sustaining people and it takes you down what is called a utilitarian path of medical ethics where we are no longer looking at the sanctity of human life and the need to preserve human life, but we are looking at these broader issues of social good and the cost to the programs.

I have not yet concluded drafting my legislation but I am pretty close. I am trying to you might say divide the baby here very accurately. It is a very, very tricky issue. My own personal experience was that most physicians get this right. We were very focused on the case of Terri Schiavo a few weeks ago. However, these kinds of decisions are made on a regular basis in most hospitals and nursing homes and hospice centers in the country and there is usually no controversy surrounding them. There is an increasing trend that I think warrants a Federal standard to be established.

Mr. CUMMINGS. Last but not least, as we get older, people living longer, I guess it is reasonable to predict that there will be more of these situations, would you agree? Is that reasonable to assume?

Dr. WELDON. Yes, I think it is quite reasonable to assume that.

Mr. CUMMINGS. I take it part of what you are saying is that we see this reverse thing going on, the withholding of food and water and we see people getting older, so therefore there is going to be more of this. We see the cost of health care going up and some kind of way in that climate, we had better prepare ourselves to set some kind of reasonable standard.

Dr. WELDON. I would describe it as a minimum moral and ethical standard that is biased toward life, in particular the fundamentals of life, food and water. I would not want to venture into the broader issue of when do you intervene with drugs or machines. Those kinds of issues I think are best left to professional associations and institutions but when you are talking about the fundamentals of food and fluid, one of the things unique about the Schiavo case is the judge's order from the bench was you could not bring a glass of water to this woman's lips. While it may seem extreme, it is not unprecedented. There have been similar cases in the past. To me that warrants what is called a substantive standard in Federal law or regulations be established regarding when it is inappropriate to do that and that standard should be biased toward life. Otherwise, we would begin going down a dangerous path of denying food and fluid to a lot of disabled people who have a will to live.

Mr. CUMMINGS. Thank you.

Mr. SOUDER. Mr. McHenry.

Mr. MCHENRY. Dr. Weldon, I certainly appreciate your testimony thus far and appreciate your depth of knowledge on this issue. I think you are in a unique position in Congress because of your medical background to address this issue.

You said a bias toward life, and this is only in cases where there is a controversy, a legal controversy about the incapacitated individual's life? Is that correct?

Dr. WELDON. No. What I am looking at is introducing legislation and I am actually soliciting input from the committee on this issue. A standard for when it is inappropriate to withdraw food and fluids really in any circumstance, not just when you have a family controversy like you had in the Schiavo case.

Mr. MCHENRY. Would this be geared directly toward Medicare or Medicaid patients?

Dr. WELDON. I would favor that and the reason I would favor that is we are the principal funder of Medicare and Medicaid and if an institution is going to receive those funds, they should be held to a standard that is biased toward giving essential nutrients and favoring a respect for human life.

Mr. MCHENRY. Is it in essence sort of a standard of case issue with Medicare and Medicaid?

Dr. WELDON. I would describe it as an extension of care issues because there are lots of standard of care issues within the Medicare and Medicaid programs that currently exist today. It is these fundamental issues or requirement of food and water have never been established before in law or in regulations.

Mr. MCHENRY. So in essence, it would be just as though Medicare and Medicaid have a certain standard of care that they demand?

Dr. WELDON. In order to be eligible to receive reimbursement through the Medicare and Medicaid program, if you are going to be taking care of these patients I think you should be held to a minimum standard of delivering food and water to people except it needs to be qualified in such a way that you are not forced to give food and fluids to people who are obviously in the dying process or people as well who have an advanced directive indicating they would not want to receive food and fluid.

Mr. MCHENRY. So in the absence of a medical directive and with the basic standard of care, so it would be an extension of current Medicare and Medicaid policy and just putting in a certain level of care that every doctor must provide for their patients?

Dr. WELDON. Correct.

Mr. MCHENRY. Thank you and thank you, Mr. Chairman, for having this hearing.

Mr. SOUDER. Ms. Brown-Waite.

Ms. BROWN-WAITE. Thank you and thank you, Doctor, for being here.

You and I have had many conversations about this very difficult issue. I would like you to clarify a couple of comments you made. One was you find it disturbing that an increasing number of doctors in hospitals unilaterally are withdrawing food and water. Could you quantify that? Is it in the tens or is it 20, is it hundreds, thousands?

Dr. WELDON. The National Right to Life Committee provided me a report and I would be very happy to make a copy of that report available to you as well as to the record. It is entitled, "Will Your Advance Directives Be Followed?" The report is full of cases where family members report advance directives in favor of administration of food and fluid were properly executed and family wishes were present that food and fluid would be continued and health care providers and institutions shut off the food and water allowing the person to die based on sometimes a medical ethics committee at the institution making the decision, sometimes it is the individual providers.

The concern I have in this is there is no standard in 80 percent of the States, in 40 States. There is no legal remedy that the family members can go to in order to prevent that from happening once the institution makes that decision. In terms of the absolute number, I can provide the report.

Ms. BROWN-WAITE. That would be very helpful.

In today's world where we have such a litigious society, doctors tell me they wouldn't do this because of fear they would be sued for either wrongful death, even though it is a premature death, or medical malpractice. I hear from doctors back in the communities that if anything, they actually are erring on the other side, putting feeding tubes in and keeping them in for the fear of litigation.

Dr. WELDON. Yes, there is some of that. Indeed, I had a very interesting conversation with a tort attorney who actually makes his living suing nursing homes. One of the things he most often sues for is failure to provide adequate food and fluids that leads to medical complications. In that same milieu, there is the other side of the story and it typically involves people with disabilities and most often it is people with severe disabilities and institutions are making decisions to withdraw food and fluid and it is typically based on a quality of life analysis. To my knowledge, none of those cases have been successfully litigated through the court system.

Ms. BROWN-WAITE. The last question for you is, if we set a standard for Medicare and Medicaid and private insurance companies don't follow it, do we have a system of unequal rights? In other words, the Medicare or Medicaid patient, we would err on the side of food and water and the private pay or one of the individual insurance companies, they would never adopt this standard. Help me to understand why we would have two standards?

Dr. WELDON. The remedy for that would be a universal Federal standard that not the Federal programs would have to adhere to but as well private insurance companies would have to adhere to it. One of the issues you would get into there if you try to move such a legislative act through the Congress is that you are usurping State authority, State law, State regulatory processes and people who hold to a very strong Federalist opinion may not want to go down that path.

My experience is the majority of these cases are within the Federal programs but your point is actually well taken and if you are alluding to the fact you would like to see it broadened, then I would be very interested in your input on that issue.

Ms. BROWN-WAITE. You sparked another question for me and that is would you have government intervention in a case similar to Terri Schiavo's where allegedly she expressed her views to people but it was never written down, so is your goal to override a family member carrying out the person who is in the hospital or in the nursing home or hospice, override their decision even if it wasn't in writing?

Dr. WELDON. What you are really getting at is if we had the standard in place during the Schiavo incident, how would that have played into the deliberations in that case?

Ms. BROWN-WAITE. Correct, because she was on Medicaid.

Dr. WELDON. Yes. I am not really sure and I would have to defer to legal scholars on that. I have not even finished the process of drafting my legislation. As you know, I am a physician, not a lawyer. It is not my intent to replay the Schiavo case in current law. What has been drawn to my attention mainly by some of the people sitting behind me who represent some of these disability groups is a strong level of concern about a trend in health care delivery which I think is being driven a lot by cost issues Mr. Cummings brought up and that you are going to see more and more people who are less and less disabled being denied care if we do not at least establish some sort of floor or basement or fundamental standard.

Ms. BROWN-WAITE. But again you would have two sets of health care, those on Medicare and Medicaid and those not covered by Medicare and Medicaid. I know you are working on a very thoughtful bill.

Dr. WELDON. I am not exactly sure what your concern would be because my experience is the Federal standards are usually adopted by private industry.

Ms. BROWN-WAITE. That may have been the case but with increasing health care costs, I am not sure unless it was mandated that insurance companies would follow through on that. I look forward to seeing your bill.

Dr. WELDON. If it was a standard in Medicare-Medicaid, it would probably involve funding and it would be targeted basically to facilities.

Mr. SOUDER. Our challenge in Congress is which rights are basic and fundamental and transcend. Is this a right to life, a right to certain types of services? Clearly in Medicaid and Medicare we make decisions and they are interpreted through the Department of Health and Human Services that are very difficult decisions. This limb constitutes this much, this limb constitutes this much and private pay can cover different things. There are different standards. The question is does the right to water and food transcend public-private, is that a basic right or is that a right tied directly to our funding? We certainly are feeling the cost pressures here. Everybody is raising health care cost questions. Businesses are raising it, doctors are raising it, hospitals are raising it, how many hearts are you entitled to, how many of this and that, how do we sort through this very difficult cost, quality of life question?

What we are saying and I think you brought up really well and hopefully we can work through this hearing is we have to be very careful about having quality of life be the sole determinant here. Are we in effect making one whole class of citizens second class citizens. Hopefully as you develop this and I know we had talked about this before the Terri Schiavo case and will continue to talk about it afterwards, but this certainly put a different heightened awareness in the case.

Thank you for coming today and testifying.

We will move to our next panel. Dr. Don Young, Deputy Assistant Secretary for Planning and Evaluation, Department of Health and Human Services whose job it is to provide as much and total health care for everybody at basically no cost and make sure everybody gets absolute service.

We do need to swear you in.

[Witness sworn.]

Mr. SOUDER. Let the record show the witness responded in the affirmative.

Thank you for taking time today to come and address. We look forward to your testimony.

STATEMENT OF DR. DONALD A. YOUNG, DEPUTY ASSISTANT SECRETARY, PLANNING AND EVALUATION, DEPARTMENT OF HEALTH AND HUMAN SERVICES

Dr. YOUNG. Thank you for inviting me today to discuss the role of Medicare, Medicaid and advanced directives for those who cannot care for themselves.

We are committed to ensuring that Medicare and Medicaid beneficiaries receive appropriate care tailored to their own needs and that they understand their rights and options in all care settings.

As the subcommittee undertakes an examination of policies regarding the status and legal rights of incapacitated individuals, I appreciate the opportunity to provide an overview of the role of the Medicare and Medicaid programs as well as other programs within the jurisdiction of the U.S. Department of Health and Human Services.

Medicare and Medicaid both play an important role in financing care for patients who may need to make choices about the types of health care they want. Medicare and Medicaid serve to protect the health of individuals at every stage of their lives, including when they cannot speak for themselves. However, decisions about health care itself are not made by Medicare and Medicaid. Such decisions are made by individuals and their families in consultation with their physicians.

The Federal Medicare and Federal State Medicaid programs provide coverage for hospital, skilled nursing facility and home health service and hospice care as well as nursing facility services for long term care for Medicare beneficiaries. Hospice covers a broad range of medical, personal assistance and social services with the goal of keeping the patient comfortable and pain free and supporting the family. Hospice was added as a benefit under the Medicare Program in 1983 and as an optional benefit under Medicaid in 1985. The number of beneficiaries electing hospice care and the number of agencies offering such services has grown steadily ever since.

The Centers for Medicare and Medicaid Services developed conditions of participation that health care organizations must meet to participate in the Medicare and Medicaid programs. These standards are used to improve quality and to protect the health and safety of beneficiaries. Conditions of participation vary by facility type and include requirements related to patient rights, medical staff, skilled nursing and rehabilitation services, food, dietetic services and needs.

An important condition of participation is the requirement regarding advance directives. The Patient Self Determination Act of 1990 requires that all adult patients in all covered settings be informed of the right to accept or refuse treatment through an advance directive. An advance directive is a written instruction such as a living will or durable power of attorney for health care. It is recognized under State law relating to the provision of health care when the individual is incapacitated. This also includes do not resuscitate orders. Compliance with this requirement is a condition of participation under the Medicare Program for hospitals, hospices, skilled nursing facilities, home health agencies and Medicare advantage plans. Medicaid managed care organizations also must comply with identical requirements.

Advance directives address both treatments individuals do and do not want. For example, an individual may prefer that health care providers perform all possible life prolonging treatments. Conversely, a person may elect to receive non-curative care. Therefore, if an individual has specific treatment preferences, they would be able to document them in an advance directive. The Social Security Act which codifies the Patient Self Determination Act of 1990 mandates that all institutions receiving Medicare and Medicare funding inform all patients regardless of whether they are entitled to Medicare and Medicaid of the right to accept or refuse medical treatment through an advance directive.

All health care institutions must maintain written policies and procedures concerning advance directives with respect to all adult individuals receiving medical care. We are required to provide written information to such individuals. In addition, providers must document in the individual's medical record whether or not the individual has executed an advance directive and may not discriminate in the provision of care to an individual based on the existence of an advance directive.

Providers must also comply with State laws regarding advance directives and provide for education of the staff and communities on issues concerning advance directives. In addition to Medicare and Medicaid, other government programs and services are available to families addressing health care issues for vulnerable individuals including Federal, State and local government partnerships that include ombudsmen protection and advocacy groups, adult and child protective services. These include the Health Resources and Services Administration programs that provide services and benefits for persons with traumatic brain injury.

The Administration on Aging has a strong commitment to protecting the rights of seniors and helping them to make end of life care decisions. Nearly 1,000 AOA funded legal providers help seniors to obtain medical and financial powers of attorney, living wills and advance directives. The AOA also administers an ombudsmen program under which local ombudsmen work on behalf of residents in hundreds of communities throughout the country. AOA also supports the National Family Care Giver Support Program.

In conclusion, we are committed to ensuring that vulnerable beneficiaries receive appropriate care through Medicare and Medicaid that is tailored to their needs and that they understand their rights and options.

As you can see, a variety of protections are in place in Medicare, Medicaid and beyond these programs to ensure that beneficiaries receive appropriate health care.

I thank you for holding this hearing and I am happy to answer your questions.

[The prepared statement of Dr. Young follows:]

Testimony of

Don Young, MD
Deputy Assistant Secretary for Planning and Evaluation
U. S. Department of Health and Human Services

Before the

House Committee on Government Reform Subcommittee on Criminal Justice, Drug Policy and Human Resources

Hearing on
Federal Health Programs and Those Who Cannot Care for Themselves: What Are Their Rights, and Our Responsibilities?

April 19, 2005

Chairman Souder, Representative Cummings, distinguished members of the Subcommittee, thank you for inviting me here today to discuss the role of Medicare, Medicaid and advance directives for those who cannot care for themselves. We are committed to ensuring that Medicare and Medicaid beneficiaries receive appropriate care tailored to their own needs and that they understand their rights and options in all care settings. As the Subcommittee undertakes an examination of policies regarding the status and legal rights of incapacitated individuals, I appreciate the opportunity to provide an overview of the role of the Medicare and Medicaid programs, as well as other programs within the jurisdiction of the U.S. Department of Health and Human Services.
Medicare and Medicaid both play an important role in financing care for patients who may need to make choices about the types of health care they want. Medicare and Medicaid serve to protect the health of individuals at every stage of their lives, including when they cannot speak for themselves. However, decisions about health care itself are not made by Medicare and Medicaid. Such decisions are made by individuals and their families in consultation with their physicians.

Medicare provides coverage for beneficiaries in hospitals, skilled nursing facilities (SNFs), home health care, and hospice care, as well as physician and outpatient services. Medicare will cover only medically necessary diagnostic and treatment services. Medicare does not pay for purely maintenance or custodial services for persons not needing medical care. For Medicaid, states may offer a variety of acute and post-acute care services for eligible individuals. Additionally, Medicaid may pay for custodial services in a variety of settings.

The Patient Self Determination Act of 1990 requires that all adult patients in all covered settings be informed of their rights under state law to accept or refuse medical treatment and the right to formulate an advance directive. According to section 1866(f) of the Social Security Act, an advance directive is "a written instruction, such as a living will or durable power of attorney for health care, recognized under State law, relating to the provision of health care when the individual is incapacitated." This also includes "do not resuscitate" (DNR) orders. Compliance with section 1866(f) is a condition of participation under the Medicare program for hospitals, hospices, skilled nursing facilities, and home health agencies. Medicare Advantage plans and Medicaid managed care organizations must also comply with identical requirements.

Enrollment and Spending under Medicare and Medicaid

Over 42 million Americans receive their health coverage through Medicare including 6.5 million beneficiaries below the age of 65 who have disabilities and about 5.1 million over the age of 65 who have limitations in three or more activities of daily living. Eight million individuals with disabilities and 4.5 million senior citizens rely on Medicaid for their health insurance and long-term care and supportive services. Many of these beneficiaries may become incapacitated and incapable of making health care decisions for themselves. Anyone, at any age, may encounter a medical crisis that may temporarily or permanently diminish his or her ability to make personal health care decisions.

Medicare and Medicaid beneficiaries receive services in a variety of settings. Medicare spent $34 billion in 2002 on post-acute care for 205,000 beneficiaries in skilled nursing facilities and $42 billion on 1.4 million full benefit dual-eligible beneficiaries in skilled nursing facilities. In 2004 the federal government and states spent $46.5 billion for approximately 1.8 million Medicaid-only beneficiaries in nursing facilities and an additional $12.1 billion on approximately 117,000 beneficiaries in intermediate care facilities for individuals with mental retardation.

In FY 2002, approximately 110,000 Medicaid enrollees received hospice care and in FY 2003, more than 640,000 Medicare beneficiaries received hospice care. Medicaid spending on hospice was approximately $700 million in FY 2002 and Medicare spending on hospice was approximately $7.2 billion in 2004. Medicare spending on hospice has grown from $1.9 billion in 1995 to an estimated $7.2 billion in 2004.

In 2000, approximately 4 million individuals annually received care in hospital intensive care or coronary care units, and it is estimated that more than half of this population were receiving either Medicare or Medicaid benefits, or both.

Facilities Offering Care for Those Who Cannot Care for Themselves

The federal Medicare and federal-state Medicaid programs cover care in a range of settings for those who cannot care for themselves. For eligible Medicare beneficiaries this includes skilled nursing facilities (SNFs) for extended care after a hospital stay and some health services at home. Under Medicaid states cover some long-term care services in nursing facilities if a beneficiary meets applicable state and federal eligibility requirements. While states are required to provide home health services for persons eligible for nursing facility services, many also have obtained waivers to make home and community-based services available to individuals who would otherwise qualify for Medicaid only if they were in an institutional setting. States also have the option to provide services through intermediate care facilities for the mentally retarded for those who are eligible.

In addition, for individuals with a terminal illness, both Medicare and Medicaid cover hospice services in facility-based settings including nursing facilities, hospitals, or other facilities and in patients' homes. Hospice covers a broad range of medical, personal assistance, and social services with the goal of keeping the patient comfortable and pain-free and supporting the family. Hospice care was added as a benefit under the Medicare program in 1983 and as an optional benefit under Medicaid in 1985. The number of beneficiaries electing hospice care, and the number of agencies offering such services, has grown steadily ever since.

To be eligible for hospice care, an individual's physician and the hospice medical director must certify that the individual is terminally ill, with approximately six months or less to live if their illness runs its normal course. Beneficiaries must sign a statement indicating that they understand that they are choosing palliative hospice care instead of routine, curative Medicare covered benefits for their terminal illness. The Medicare and Medicaid programs recognize that terminal illnesses do not have entirely predictable courses; therefore, if the patient surpasses the initial six-month prognosis, the beneficiary may remain eligible for hospice if the individual's physician and hospice medical director recertify that the patient has a life expectancy of six months or less.

CMS develops Conditions of Participation (CoPs) and Conditions for Coverage (CfCs) that health care organizations must meet to participate in the Medicare and Medicaid programs. These standards are used to improve quality and protect the health and safety of beneficiaries. CMS also ensures that the standards of accrediting organizations recognized by CMS (through a process called "deeming") meet or exceed Medicare standards. CoPs vary by facility-type (e.g. nursing facilities and skilled nursing facilities) and include a vast number of conditions related to, for example, patient rights, medical staff, skilled nursing and rehabilitation services, and food and dietetic services. However, one CoP that is applicable to most facilities is the requirement regarding advance directives.

Advance Directives

It is important for individuals to know how advance directives can ensure that they receive the kind of care they choose. Living wills specify individuals' desired medical decisions if they are incapacitated and cannot speak for themselves. Proxy appointments and durable powers of attorney for health care designate a third party to make medical decisions if an individual becomes incapacitated.

Advance directives address both treatments individuals do and do not want. For example, an individual may prefer that health care providers perform all possible life-prolonging treatments. Conversely, a person may elect to receive non-curative care. Therefore, if an individual has specific treatment preferences, they would be able to document them in an advance directive.

Provider Requirements

Sections 1866(a)(1)(Q) and 1866(f) of the Social Security Act, which codify the Patient Self Determination Act of 1990, mandate that most institutions receiving Medicare and Medicaid funding inform all adult patients – regardless of whether they are entitled to Medicare or Medicaid – of their right to accept or refuse medical treatment through an advance directive. Most health care institutions must maintain written policies and procedures concerning advance directives with respect to all adult individuals receiving medical care, and are required to provide written information to such individuals concerning the following.

- o An individual's rights under state law (whether statutory or recognized by the courts of the state) to make decisions concerning such medical care
- o The written policies of the provider or organization respecting the implementation of such rights, including a clear and precise statement of limitation if the provider cannot implement an advance directive on the basis of conscience

In addition, providers must document in the individual's medical record whether or not the individual has executed an advance directive and may not discriminate in the provision of care to an individual based on the existence of an advance directive. Providers must also comply with state law regarding advance directives, and provide for education of the staff and communities on issues concerning advance directives.

Other Types of Beneficiary Protections

In addition to Medicare and Medicaid, other government programs and services are available to families addressing health care issues for vulnerable individuals, including federal, state, and local government partners that include ombudsmen, protection and advocacy groups, adult protective services, and child protective services. These include the Health Resources and Services Administration programs that provide services for persons with traumatic brain injury. More specifically, the Administration on Aging (AoA) has a strong commitment to protecting the rights of seniors and helping them when they need to make end-of-life care decisions.

Survey and Certification

The Survey and Certification Group in CMS' Center for Medicaid and State Operations is responsible for overseeing the programs established to monitor quality of care and ensure beneficiary protections within the Medicare and Medicaid programs; for ensuring that corrective action is taken when problems are found; and for ensuring that beneficiaries receive quality care in a safe environment.

CMS' requirement that providers initially meet eligibility qualifications and recertify to ensure continued compliance is intended to protect beneficiaries. Furthermore, CMS conducts complaint investigations of facilities in response to beneficiary concerns about care. As an example, approximately 6,000 Federal and state surveyors conducted on-site reviews of nursing facilities. On average, skilled nursing facilities are surveyed every 12 months, home health every three years, and hospice every six years. In addition to the role of the Survey and Certification Group, CMS provides beneficiaries with online tools, including Nursing Facility Compare, Hospital Compare, and Home Health Compare so that they and their caregivers can make informed decisions about long-term and other care services.

Administration on Aging (AoA) Programs to Prevent Elder Abuse

AoA has a range of programs available that allow millions of seniors to age in place with dignity. AoA also supports a range of activities at the state and local level designed to prevent elder fraud and abuse and inform seniors of their rights. These activities include training law enforcement officers and medical professionals in how to recognize and respond to elder abuse cases, conducting public awareness and education campaigns, and creating statewide and local elder abuse prevention coalitions and multi-disciplinary teams.

National Family Caregiver Support Program (NFCSP)

The enactment of the Older Americans Act Amendments of 2000 established an important new program, the National Family Caregiver Support Program (NFCSP). The program was developed by AoA and was modeled in large part after successful state programs (i.e. California, New Jersey, Wisconsin, and Pennsylvania). The program calls for all states, working in partnership with local area agencies on aging and faith- and community-based service providers and tribes, to offer five direct services that best meet the range of caregivers' needs, including:

- Information to caregivers about available services;
- Assistance to caregivers in gaining access to supportive services;
- Individual counseling, organization of support groups, and caregiver training to assist caregivers in making decisions and solving problems relating to their roles;

- Respite care to enable caregivers to be temporarily relieved from their caregiving responsibilities; and
- Supplemental services, on a limited basis, to complement the care provided by caregivers.

AoA developed a fact sheet that explains the services provided by hospices and how to find information on the financial, legal, and after-death responsibilities that families must address.

Ombudsman Program

The AoA also administers an ombudsman program under which local ombudsmen work on behalf of residents in hundreds of communities throughout the country. Long-term care ombudsmen are advocates for residents of nursing facilities, board and care homes, assisted living facilities and similar adult care facilities. Since the program began 30 years ago, thousands of paid and volunteer ombudsmen have made a dramatic difference in the lives of long-term care residents. Ombudsmen advocate on behalf of individuals and groups of residents, provide information to residents and their families about the long-term care system, and work to effect systems changes on a local, state and national level. They provide an on-going presence in long-term care facilities, monitoring care and conditions and providing a voice for those who are unable to speak for themselves.

AoA also serves as a resource for those who need help in making decisions regarding long-term care. Information on hospice, living wills, advanced directives, palliative care, advocacy, and professional information is provided on the AoA's website (www.aoa.gov).

Advocacy and Support Organizations

A number of organizations are dedicated to helping people address end-of-life issues. For example, AoA has worked closely with the National Hospice and Palliative Care Organization to provide information on hospice and palliative care services. Such organizations work to improve the quality of services available, as well as provide information and resources on related issues, such as advanced directives and living wills.

Nearly 1,000 AoA-funded legal providers help seniors to obtain medical and financial powers of attorney, living wills, and advance directives (combination of a medical power of attorney and a living will). These legal tools prevent unnecessary guardianships and help seniors to make informed end-of-life decisions. AoA funded the American Bar Association Commission on Law and Aging to create English and Spanish versions of the guide "Health and Financial Decisions: Legal Tools for Preserving Your Personal Autonomy."

Conclusion

We are committed to ensuring that vulnerable beneficiaries receive appropriate care through Medicare and Medicaid that is tailored to their needs and that they understand their rights and options. Mr. Chairman, as you can see, a variety of protections are in place in Medicare, Medicaid, and beyond these programs to ensure that beneficiaries receive appropriate health care. I thank you for holding this hearing, and I am happy to answer your questions.

Mr. SOUDER. Let me see if I understand this correctly. The medical decision whether to spend the money, the Medicare-Medicaid money, is made at the doctor or hospital level and you don't monitor this unless someone makes a complaint?

Dr. YOUNG. No. Let me make a very important clarification here. I was speaking of the conditions of participation. The Medicare Program sets those conditions of participation and surveys facilities to be sure they are adhering to those conditions of participation. One of the requirements within those conditions of participation is the requirement they offer an advance directive. The Medicare and Medicaid programs set similar policies related to reimbursement to which your question was directed.

Once conditions have been set for reimbursement, once decisions have been made on what is a covered service and what is not a covered service, if the physician is furnishing it in a way that meets professional standards, we don't get into the examining room between the physician and the patient.

Mr. SOUDER. What did you think of Dr. Weldon's statement which he said came from a right to life report that many hospitals, up to 80 percent, have often violated the express will of the patient and is there monitoring of this?

Dr. YOUNG. I was first of all surprised by that. I had not seen that report. I intend to obtain that report and look at it very soon. Amongst the kinds of questions I had were if indeed there were 80 percent, was it 1 patient out of 1,000. That is, did something happen that could have been inadvertent or willful? We have some information related to nursing homes. We do not have a lot of good information on this. A substantial proportion of nursing homes are following the rules but not all of them and there are times we have to go in and cite and encourage them to adhere to the rules they say they are adhering to.

Mr. SOUDER. Do you know of any cases where you have intervened in a feeding type situation?

Dr. YOUNG. The Department or the Medicare Program?

Mr. SOUDER. Yes, where there was somebody who had a statement, the hospital didn't want to provide it and the Department of HHS has intervened and said look you are supposed to provide that either by fining them or rebuking them? Do you have a penalty if they don't?

Dr. YOUNG. First of all, I am not aware of that having occurred. In terms of our conditions of participation and our overall requirements, we do have surveys and we do check. There are penalties that are on institutions for violations of those. They can be civil money penalties, monetary but for very egregious violations of conditions of participation, providers can lose their ability to participate in Medicare and Medicaid which essentially effects their providing services to everybody.

Mr. SOUDER. Are almost all of those cases brought to your attention by the system you set up for elder abuse reporting or disability reporting, national family care giver support programs or are these being found and discovered by HHS investigators?

Dr. YOUNG. They are being found by either the staff responsible for drafting and enforcing the standards and frequently that is done at the regional office level not centrally.

Mr. SOUDER. You had in your full written statement that according to the Patient Self-Determination Act of 1990, it mandated that most institutions receiving Medicare and Medicaid funding inform all adult patients. What would be the exception category, do you know?

Dr. YOUNG. All of what we call providers and provider facilities are covered by that—hospices, nurses, skilled nursing facility, long-term care hospitals, acute care hospitals. All those things that we would call an institutional provider plus a hospice, which may be without walls, are covered by that.

Mr. SOUDER. I would be interested in your personal reaction, since you are a physician as well, to what I asked Congressman Weldon about the U.S. Conference of Bishops. I know you were here and heard the question about this difficult question that, practically speaking, how is a decision reached that a procedure has no medically reasonable hope of sustaining life or poses excessive risks or burdens, and should this consideration override Federal presumption in support of nutrition and hydration?

Dr. YOUNG. There are some very, very difficult judgments embedded in that. When a patient looks like they are end of life, you can look at their brain functioning, you can do a whole host of studies and tests to see is there any probability of recovery here. If they have advanced diseases such as cancer, you know approximately what their life frame is. Having all that information, that still boils down to an extremely difficult decision to be made.

And if you are talking about some of the things we were talking about here today, the physician needs to involve the family and know the family's wishes and the patient's wishes. If you do not have an advanced directive, and it would be nice if you always had one, then you have to have some understanding what you and the family believe the patient would have wanted and what they would have wanted. And your concern, ultimately, is still the welfare of the patient. So, as Dr. Weldon said, there is a time when there is severe suffering and that has to be a factor you and the family consider in making your determination.

Mr. SOUDER. Thank you. Mr. Cummings.

Mr. CUMMINGS. If the problems that Dr. Weldon talked about that he read in the Right to Life document that he just referred to a moment ago, if that were something that were happening—and I am not saying it is not, I do not know—who would know that? It seems like that is the kind of information that would come to some office in HHS. Is that reasonable to guess?

Dr. YOUNG. Let us assume that there have been violations and there are more than random violations, which you may not find, the patient, the patient's family can report it, they can report it to one of the various hotlnes, they can report it to the IG, they can report it to HHS directly. Providers in that hospital could discover it and report it via one of those mechanisms. Routine audits of medical records could determine it and it could be reported through the hospital's own quality oversight and medical audit review, professional standards review organizations. There are numerous places within the health care system where there is oversight that hopefully would identify and report up that kind of problem.

The question I have that you are going to have to ask the legal authority, Justice Department, is, if, indeed, these determinations have been made by the patient, how can they be overturned by the hospital? And I do not have enough detail to understand that report from Dr. Weldon. But I think embedded in that is a very important legal question that needs to be answered as well, if, indeed, that is happening more than on rare occasions.

Mr. CUMMINGS. So I would take it, based upon what you just said, that you were a bit surprised by that comment of Congressman Weldon that this was something that apparently has happened quite a bit. Were you surprised?

Dr. YOUNG. Yes, sir, I was surprised. I am not aware of that report.

Mr. CUMMINGS. OK. You prepared a statement to come here today, did you not, and it is a very good statement. I was just wondering, I know it may have caught you by surprise what he said, but in your discussions with the people in your office, I am sure you had discussions generally, did you hear about anything like this?

Dr. YOUNG. No.

Mr. CUMMINGS. One of the things that Dr. Weldon said that I think just deserves a lot of consideration is he talked about whether you are prolonging life or prolonging the death process. And you have said it to a degree, that this is a judgment, this is a pretty significant judgment call. I am just wondering, the chairman asked you about monitoring and how is it monitored, I would guess that even if you were doing some monitoring, there might at this point be some question as to—let us say you have somebody who says, look, that doctor withheld water and food and it was a directive of my loved one to have everything possible to sustain my life, food and water to save my life. Is there not a question then, is this sustaining the life, or is this sustaining the death?

Dr. YOUNG. You put your finger on an extraordinarily not only complex, but very, very difficult judgment. The body is a very, very resilient thing and predicting how different people will react under differing circumstances, even those who are very, very sick, is very difficult and fraught with error.

Mr. CUMMINGS. When I practiced law, we often had to have guardianships over people because they could not do for themselves, and quite often dementia set in. When you are trying to figure out what is in the best interests of this person, it does become a bit complicated. One of the standards has been that you want to do everything you can do to protect the person, almost like you would protect a baby, because they cannot protect themselves.

So, in this instance, it seems as if one of the things that we are trying to do, and I think—I think—part of the reason for this hearing is to protect those who are most vulnerable and those who find themselves in a situation because of illness or what have you where they cannot—well, it depends, if they made a decision, trying to carry out that decision, if they have not made the decision, trying to figure out what you do from there. Do you think there is enough in the law right now to protect people, you following me, with what you are familiar with?

Dr. YOUNG. Yes. Yes, I do follow you. I understand the question. I think the most important protections that are there are through the Medicare conditions of participation that apply to everybody, and that is the requirements related to an advanced directive. The deficiency that we have, and I think it applies to all of us, is we probably need to do a better job educating the public to fill out those papers and to do their advanced directives, because we still have a substantial number of people who have not. If we had those advanced directives for everybody, if the loved ones, the family, the physicians knew the wishes, then the kinds of decisions and discussions that we are talking about today would be very rare and might not be there at all.

Mr. CUMMINGS. I was just reading and listening to what you had to say about the ombudsman. They play a pretty significant role. How prevalent are they, doctor, the ombudsmen? It seems like a really wonderful position. I see some of them are voluntary, so I do not know how widespread they are. Are they controlled, by the way, do we have anything under HHS that sets any criteria for ombudsmen, what they are supposed to do, what they are supposed to be looking for? Or is it just something where people kind come into hospitals or hospices and say, look, I am volunteering, I want to just kind of watch over things. Because I am wondering, if it is not something that is pretty concrete, maybe that is something that we might want to look into.

Dr. YOUNG. They are voluntary. But the program itself is one that I do not have the details on, I would be happy to get you more information and submit it for the record.

Mr. CUMMINGS. But from what you have written here, I am almost finished, Mr. Chairman, they do and can play a significant role. As a matter of fact, it sounds like they could possibly play the role of a whistle-blower at times. Is that reasonable to conclude?

Dr. YOUNG. Well, yes. And there is not one single ombudsman or ombudsman program. There are people out there who are very interested in Medicare beneficiaries, there are centers who are funded to look at, to help, and to provide advice and guidance to Medicare's beneficiaries with problems, help intercede on their behalf. But I will get you more information.

Mr. CUMMINGS. Last, but not least, what would you like to see us do, if anything? Can you think of anything? You know the subject matter here, what we are looking at. Do you see loopholes? We are trying to figure out how we can help in this process to clarify or to draw the line. Do you have any recommendations about any of this?

Dr. YOUNG. Yes. I have listened carefully to the proceedings so far, to Dr. Weldon. I do not have any suggestions and recommendations. A lot of this is very much personal that belongs with the family, with the doctor, with the patient's wishes. If you identify something that you think would be the appropriate subject of Federal legislation, we would be happy to look at it, give you our opinion and our advice.

Mr. CUMMINGS. OK. Thank you.

Mr. SOUDER. One thing that would help as a start, our staff tried to get data under Medicare and Medicaid as to any numbers that you might have on people in minimally conscious state or persistent vegetative state that are funded under Medicare or Medicaid. We do not have any idea of the universe of people we are dealing with. Is this a little problem? A big problem? Does such data exist?

Dr. YOUNG. We have some limited data. On the Medicaid program side, there was a study done, it is probably 4 years, 5 years old now, but under that study, it was estimated there were about 2,500 people accountable for about $600 million in spending for inpatient care with a diagnosis of persistent vegetative state. So that gives you some notion. It is not an inconsequential number of people or an inconsequential number of dollars, and that is only for the inpatient hospital setting. Were that done in nursing homes, you would certainly find additional increase.

Mr. SOUDER. So you do not have reporting data that would isolate that? That was a study done, a sampling?

Dr. YOUNG. Yes. All of this would have to be done either as a study using claims data, or as a research project that was designed specifically to get at the questions that are being asked.

Mr. SOUDER. Because one of the things, in addition to this group of individuals, really, what is underneath the concern here is, as we grapple with incredibly intense cost pressures, from our funding level that is going to HHS, to the State level, flat funding Medicaid all over the country as we block grant more to them, that the goal of hospitals and nursing homes is to cap the number of Medicare and Medicaid patients that they have and try to blend it as much with at least private payer, blend it and this cost pressure. What we have as a fundamental concern here is that those who are least able to speak for themselves and those with disabilities are going to get shunted aside or at least have less of a voice.

There needs to be a fair public debate about how we are going to resolve this difficult question. Because they probably take a lot of dollars per patient, for a long period of time, have, depending on the nature of their disability, more specialists involved, and, therefore, become vulnerable, especially if their spouses or children may not live in the area, may not be alive. So how do we as a society make these kinds of decisions? And if we do not have some basic data in addition to casual sampling, the pressure—let us say if there is a hospital that is already cost-squeezed and there are 10 patients at that hospital as opposed to none at a private pay hospital, how do we sort through, and what is our responsibility as a Nation to protect individuals' fundamental rights, like we did under ADA or other types of legislation?

Dr. YOUNG. I very much agree with you, Mr. Chairman, on the problem with costs. We, as a Nation, are struggling with that. I think we will continue to struggle with it. But we need to do something about that because of the downside in terms of numbers of people who are uninsured and other issues.

In terms of health care spending, we have always spent the most on the sickest. Twenty-seven percent of Medicare's expenditures are for people in the last year of life. Now having said that, let me add very quickly a large of amount of expenditures are also for people who live longer than that year. And it is a very slippery slope if you start to raise this issue. This spending does not occur once, and people frequently do not get into a condition where they are on life support tubes as a single event. It can happen, you are very healthy, you go into the hospital, you need to have breathing assistance after surgery, then something else happens and you need to have food and water, then something else happens and you need to have kidney dialysis. This occurs over time. It is not a one-time kind of thing and that spending occurs over time. So we put, as a Nation, and in the Medicare program, a large amount of our resources on the very sickest people, and that is appropriate.

Mr. SOUDER. I want to reiterate again, unless we have data, it is tough to monitor. I know you have all kinds of pressure to get all kinds of data, too, and we have reams of it stacked that nobody ever looks at. It is one of the favorite things of Congress to do is ask for data and then have nobody look at it, or find it so inaccessible that you cannot find what you are looking for. Nevertheless, this type of question, in addition to the occasional study, if we are going to make sure, otherwise, we are, in fact, dependent on the ombudsman and the occasional kind of whistle-blower calling this, because we cannot really do oversight, we cannot really do planning in the agency or in Congress if we do not know how many we are dealing with, what percentage of cost that is other than in a random study, which may, in fact, be enough if the studies are accurate and repetitive enough.

Dr. YOUNG. I understand your point, Mr. Chairman, and I will certainly carry it back to the Department to the various components that are involved in doing research and analysis.

Mr. SOUDER. Otherwise, we could pass legislation that is so sweeping but not be relevant.

Dr. YOUNG. I agree with you. I do policy primarily for a living, and data research and analysis is the core tool for our work.

Mr. SOUDER. Ms. Watson, did you have any questions of this witness?

Ms. WATSON. No. I will pass.

Mr. CUMMINGS. I have one other.

Mr. SOUDER. Mr. Cummings.

Mr. CUMMINGS. Just one question. I just missed that 20-some percent you said. What was that, last year?

Dr. YOUNG. Yes, 27 percent of Medicare's expenditures were for people during the last year of their life.

Mr. CUMMINGS. Twenty-seven percent?

Dr. YOUNG. Yes. But a very large number are for people who do not die that year but continue to live. It is very risky to look at this and say, gee, 27 percent go to people who die, because you also know that 27 percent go to people who do not die. You have to look at both pieces of that spending. There are very sick people who live, and there are very sick people who die in a given year.

Mr. CUMMINGS. As we look, going back to something I asked Congressman Weldon, as we look at the fact that we are living longer, at HHS, are you all paying attention to that? It seems like it would be almost impossible for you not to be. Because based upon what you just said, people are living longer and we are spending 27 percent of our Medicare dollars in the last year of life, and you have more people you are doing that for. And I understand all you said about some live and some do not. So what are you all doing?

Dr. YOUNG. Much of that work is being done through the National Institutes on Aging. They have done a great deal of work; they have ongoing studies. Amongst the findings, for example, are as the population has gotten older, the age at which people become disabled or limited has also moved out dramatically. So the 65 year old person today continues to work and contribute to society. Twenty years ago, the probability of that was less. There are people now 75 and 80 who are very, very healthy. So old age by itself, however you want to define that, is frequently associated with very robust life.

Mr. CUMMINGS. I have to tell you, old age is a moving target. The older you get, the more it moves. [Laughter.]

Dr. YOUNG. We want to keep it moving out.

Mr. CUMMINGS. Thank you.

Mr. SOUDER. Thank you very much for your testimony. We may have some followup. I wanted to clarify for the record, the Right to Life report said that 80 percent of the States do not have laws effectively protecting against hospital denial of food and fluids. That is different than saying 80 percent had not done that. That is a substantially different statistic.

Dr. YOUNG. Yes, sir. Thank you, sir.

Mr. SOUDER. Thank you for testifying today.

If our third panel could come forth; Diane Coleman, Bob Sedlmeyer, Kate Adamson, and Robert Destro.

I will administer the oath.

[Witnesses sworn.]

Mr. SOUDER. Let the record show that each of the witnesses responded in the affirmative.

We are going to start with Diane Coleman, who is president of Not Dead Yet. Thank you for coming today, and we appreciate your testimony.

STATEMENTS OF DIANE COLEMAN, PRESIDENT, NOT DEAD YET; BOB SEDLMEYER, FORT WAYNE, IN; KATE ADAMSON, REDONDO BEACH, CA; AND ROBERT DESTRO, PROFESSOR, COLUMBUS SCHOOL OF LAW, THE CATHOLIC UNIVERSITY OF AMERICA

STATEMENT OF DIANE COLEMAN

Ms. Coleman. Thank you. Thanks for the opportunity to talk with you today. I have a J.D. and an MBA from UCLA, and I am on the adjunct faculty at the University of Illinois at Chicago, coteaching a graduate course series in disability and medical ethics. I am also the executive director of Progress Center for Independent Living in Forest Park, IL, which is a nonprofit service and advocacy center operated by and for people with disabilities.

I have a neuromuscular disability and I have used a motorized wheelchair since I was 11. The first thing I would like to do, because of the topic of this hearing, is to acknowledge Congressman Danny Davis, who is also a member of this committee, for his leadership in cosponsoring MiCASSA, the Medicaid Community Attendant Services and Supports Act, which would give people with disabilities, old and young, the choice to receive long term care services in their own homes rather than being forced into more expensive and dehumanizing nursing homes and other institutions against their will. For an indepth discussion of that, I refer you to the testimony of Bob Kafka which was submitted in writing for this hearing. I am sure it is over on the table there. I hope that you and many of your colleagues will become cosponsors of this important legislation.

When I was 6 years old, my doctor told my parents that I would die by the age of 12. I am 52, so, so much for predictions. But 3 years ago, I started using a breathing machine at night. I had two friends about a decade ago, one was in her 30's and one was in her 50's, who needed the same thing. But their doctors, who were in Nashville at major hospitals, discouraged them from it without really saying what would happen as a result. At an early age, they each went into respiratory distress, and died each within a month of that from infections. I have had many friends say they were pressured to sign do not resuscitate orders, and some who said the doctor told they are under one whether they like it or not, hospital policy.

Frankly, I am a bit worried about what might happen to me if I get into some kind of a medical crisis and wind up in a hospital. I have a health care proxy, but I am worried that his decisions that I have entrusted to him might not be followed. I am not at all convinced that decisions to live are still treated with the same respect as decisions to die.

By the time the Schiavo case reached major national attention, 26 national disability organizations had said that Terri Schiavo should receive food and water, that her rights had not been protected, she had not selected her own guardian, the evidence was so conflicted it did not meet Constitutional standards. So I have attached to my written testimony a 3-page statement that was issued by 23 of those organizations in October 2003, and also a more recent article co-authored by Steve Eidelman, who is the head of the Arc of the United States, formerly known as the Association for Retarded Citizens, and Steven Drake, who is research analyst for Not Dead Yet.

We have wondered by pro-life and religious groups have received so much attention while so many prominent disability organizations have been ignored. It appears that disability rights advocates do not fit a script that the media and many others have seemed determined to follow. For the last three decades, certain bioethicists have told you that euthanasia is about compassionate progressives versus the religious right. Never mind that these bioethicists are actually talking about the legal parameters for statutory guardians and health care providers to medically end the lives of people with disabilities on a discriminatory, non-voluntary or outright involuntary basis. Concerned disability groups do not fit the script and so we have been ignored.

The bioethicists who have shaped this debate apparently think of themselves as progressives, but they never seem to discuss cutting unnecessary health care marketing costs or profits before cutting lives. People with disabilities would like to educate them about the difference between a dying person and a person with a disability who is nowhere near death but depends on medical treatment to live.

We have a lot of information and arguments and we have tried to put them forth—in fact, we filed three amicus briefs in the Schiavo case—but, again, we are ignored. Many of these bioethicists have actually had hundreds of millions of dollars to work with over the last 15 years from major foundations, and they have used it to build a steamroller that is decimating the civil and Constitutional rights of people in guardianship. They have been making rules about who lives and who dies, changing State laws state-by-state, influencing attorneys general state-by-state, and Hollywood screenwriters, all of this pretty much behind closed doors and under the public radar screen. We agree that many things are private family matters, like parental discipline of children, for example, until they go too far.

Is there a Federal role? I think the disability community feels that there is. It is a civil rights issue. It is one of those States rights can be States wrongs kinds of things. But we do agree that there are a lot of complexities, a lot of people affected by this, a lot of experiences that people have had that influence how they feel about it. And we feel that we need to be very deliberate and proceed carefully, not in a rush, but rather to come together and figure out how best to honor and respect all individuals. So, in a way, we feel like we need a time out.

The ideas of collecting information are really useful. It is kind of shocking that the Cruzan opinion came out in 1990 and somehow, with all those hundreds of studies of advanced directives and hundreds more of so many other things relating to so-called end of life care, some end of life care is good, but others is more about ending lives, and we are trying to figure out the difference here, but with all those studies, we do not know who is dying by withholding of treatment, who made the decision, what treatments were withheld, under what circumstances. We do not even know that for people in Medicare and Medicaid. And we could not even go back and do a retrospective study of medical records because the cause of death is written as whatever the underlying condition is and not the withholding of treatment. So it is going to have to be a very deliberate process that figures this thing out.

Regardless of our abilities or disabilities, none of us should feel that we have to die to have dignity or be relieved of pain, or that we should have to die to stop burdening our families or society. We would like all of this committee to reject the script, the right-left script. Listen to the disability rights movement. On that issue of the coming wave of aging baby-boomers, we are your advanced guard. We have been doing this for decades, working out what are the ways to best deal with empowering individuals and families and supporting individuals and families to live to their highest potential, and in a way that is as cost-effective and consumer-directed as possible. That is what we are about. We would like to help everybody figure out how to do that in time that a decade or two from now we will be glad who we turned out to be.

[The prepared statement of Ms. Coleman follows:]

Testimony Before the Subcommittee on
Criminal Justice, Drug Policy and Human Resources
Of the Committee on Government Reform
Of the U.S. House of Representatives

Oversight Hearing on
"Federal Health Programs and
Those Who Cannot Care for Themselves:
What Are Their Rights,
And Our Responsibilities?"

April 19, 2005

Diane Coleman, J.D.
President
Not Dead Yet
7521 Madison Street
Forest Park, IL 60130
708-209-1500 ext. 11
Fax 708-209-1735
Email: ndycoleman@aol.com
www.notdeadyet.org

Mr. Chairman, Vice-Chairman, members, thank you for the opportunity to address this Subcommittee. My name is Diane Coleman. I have a Juris Doctorate and Masters in Business Administration from the University of California at Los Angeles, and am a member of the California bar, on inactive status. During the last twenty years, I have been employed first as an attorney for the State of California, then as Co-Director of an assistive technology center in Nashville, Tennessee, and now I am the Executive Director of Progress Center for Independent Living in Forest Park, Illinois, a nonprofit nonresidential service and advocacy center operated by and for people with disabilities.

I have had a neuromuscular disability since birth, and have used a motorized wheelchair since the age of eleven. From 1987 through 1995, I volunteered as a national organizer for ADAPT, also known as the American Disabled for Attendant Programs Today. I continue to advocate, speak and guest lecture on long-term care issues within Illinois.

In April, 1996, I founded Not Dead Yet, a national grassroots disability rights organization opposing the legalization of assisted suicide and euthanasia. I have twice presented invited testimony before the Constitution Subcommittee of the Judiciary Committee of the U.S. House of Representatives (April 29, 1996 and July 14, 1998) on the topic of assisted suicide. Over the last decade, I have appeared regarding assisted suicide and euthanasia on *Nightline, CBS Up To the Minute, ABC World News Tonight, CNN, Court TV, CBS Evening News, MSNBC's The Abrahms Report, Fox News* and *National Public Radio, among others.* I co-authored Amicus Briefs filed in the U.S. Supreme Court on behalf of Not Dead Yet and ADAPT in the matter of *Vacco* v. *Quill* (1996) and in the *Conservatorship of the Person of Robert Wendland* in the California Supreme Court (2000). In 2003, I joined the adjunct faculty at the University of Illinois at Chicago to co-teach a series of graduate courses in disability and medical ethics.

First, I would like to thank Congressman Danny Davis for his leadership in sponsoring MiCASSA, the Medicaid Community Attendant Services and Supports Act, which would give people with disabilities, old and young, the choice to receive long term care services in their own homes rather than being forced, for lack of alternatives, into more expensive and dehumanizing nursing homes and institutions. For an in-depth substantive discussion of MiCASSA and Money Follows the Person legislation, I would like to refer you to the written testimony of Bob Kafka submitted for this hearing. I hope that many more of you, from both sides of the aisle, will soon add your names as co-sponsors of this important proposal.

When I was six years old, my doctor told my parents that I would not live past the age of 12. A few years later, the diagnosis changed and so did my life expectancy. Over time, I learned that respiratory issues would probably develop. I have friends who've used nighttime ventilators for years, so I knew what symptoms to watch for, and three years ago, started using a breathing machine at night. I had two other friends in Nashville, one in her 30's and one in her 50's, who needed the same thing. But their doctors discouraged them from it, reinforcing their fears, and either didn't know or didn't disclose what the medical journals said would happen as a result. At an early age, they each went into respiratory distress, and died within a month from infections. A number of my other friends have been pressured by hospital employees to sign do-not-resuscitate orders and other advance directives to forego treatment, coupled with negative statements about how bad it would be if they became more disabled. Frankly, I'm becoming worried about what might happen to me in a hospital if I have a heart attack or other medical crisis. I have appointed my health care proxy, but will the decisions I have entrusted to him be followed by my health care providers? I am not at all convinced that decisions to live are any longer treated with the same respect by health care providers as decisions to die. In fact, I am sure they are not.

Nine years ago, I was on my way to testify before the House Constitution Subcommittee about the opposition to legalized assisted suicide coming from national disability rights organizations. Many of us were worried about Jack Kevorkian, whose body count was 70% people with non-terminal disabilities, and we were worried about two Circuit Courts declaring assisted suicide a constitutional right. We had begun to think that we needed a street action group like ADAPT to address the problem, and it was actually the head of ADAPT who thought of our name, taken from a running gag in Monty Python and The Holy Grail, Not Dead Yet. From our viewpoint, assisted suicide laws would create a dangerous double standard for society's response to suicidal expressions, an unequal response depending on one's health or disability status, with physicians as gatekeepers. That sounds like deadly discrimination to us and, frankly, we've been disappointed that the U.S. Dept. of Justice didn't use our civil rights law, the Americans With Disabilities Act, to challenge the Oregon assisted suicide law. Like other minority groups, we feel that discrimination is best addressed on the federal level, and states rights have too often meant states wrongs. To date, eleven other national disability rights organizations have adopted Not Dead Yet's position opposing legalized assisted suicide.

It wasn't long before the problem of non-voluntary and involuntary withdrawal of food and water also moved onto Not Dead Yet's radar screen. Before Terri Schiavo, there was Robert Wendland in California. Both his wife and mother agreed that Mr. Wendland was not in a persistent vegetative state, and that he had not left clear and convincing evidence of his wishes. Nevertheless, his wife argued that she should be able to remove his tube feeding anyway, and Dr. Ron Cranford was on the scene to support her. A state statute, based on a national model health care decisions code, gave her the right to starve and dehydrate him, and forty-three bioethicists filed a friend of the court brief in agreement. Ten disability rights organizations filed against the general presumption that no one would want to live with his disabilities, being used to justify lowering constitutional protections of his life. Ultimately, the California Supreme Court agreed with us that his life could not be taken without clear and convincing evidence of his wishes.

By the time the Schiavo case reached major national attention in 2003, twenty-six national disability organizations had taken a position that Terri Schiavo should receive food and water, due to the highly conflicting evidence of her wishes and the fact that she had not chosen her own guardian. Attached to my written testimony is a three page statement issued by twenty-three such groups in October 2003, and a more recent article co-authored by Steve Eidelman, head of the Arc of the United States, and Stephen Drake, research analyst for Not Dead Yet. We were deeply disturbed to see court after court uphold questionable lower court rulings. This time, 55 bioethicists supported the removal of food and water. We were also disturbed that the court allowed most of Terri Schiavo's rehabilitation funds to be spent on her husband's lawyers, that she was denied a properly fitted wheelchair, a swallowing test, swallowing therapy, the potential for oral feeding, speech therapy, and the freedom to leave the hospice with her parents, even temporarily. And we were concerned that adult protective services did not intervene, and the state protection and advocacy agency tried but proved powerless. It would appear that the prevalent prejudice that no one would want to live like Terri Schiavo translated into her guardian's unfettered right to treat her at best as a prisoner, at worst as though she was already dead.

Nevertheless, the perspectives of such prominent national groups as The Arc of the United States (formerly the Association for retarded Citizens), the National Spinal Cord Injury Association, the National Council on Independent Living, and many others were consistently ignored by most of the press, as well as the courts.

Unfortunately, the anecdotal evidence suggests that Terri Schiavo's case may be the tip of a very large and almost fully submerged iceberg. I've been a health care advocate for a couple decades, often joining street protests against government health cuts. One mission of the end-of-life care movement is a good one, to educate health care providers about how to provide good palliative care, but another mission is to shape public policy on health care. It appears that a certain line of thought in bioethics has pretty much taken over the policy-making work. This line of thought involves a lifeboat approach, deciding who gets thrown out.

When we analyze, why have the pro-life and religious advocates received such disproportionate attention, we are forced to conclude that disability rights advocates don't fit a script that everyone else seems determined to follow. For the last three decades, certain bioethicists have told the press and the public that euthanasia is about compassionate progressives versus the religious right. Never mind that these bioethicists are actually talking about the legal parameters for statutory guardians and health care providers to medically end the lives of people with disabilities on a discriminatory, non-voluntary or involuntary basis. Never mind that it takes more documentation to dispose of our property than to dispose of our lives. Concerned disability groups don't fit the script and so we have been marginalized or ignored entirely.

Here's how I'm beginning to look at things. The far right wants to kill us slowly and painfully by cutting the things we need to live, health care, public housing and transportation, etc. The far left wants to kill us quickly and call it compassion, while also saving money for others perhaps deemed more worthy.

The lifeboat bioethicists who have shaped this debate apparently think of themselves as progressives, but they never seem to discuss cutting unnecessary health care marketing costs or profits before cutting lives. My sister recently started a new career as a medical assistant at a practice with 25 doctors in Michigan. She said that four days out of five, she doesn't have to buy lunch because it's catered in by pharmaceutical companies. Marketing costs. But rather than spending all that professional brain power on conquering the waste and inhumanity of a profit-driven health care system, these bioethicists are pushing new health care decisions laws to kill disabled people who aren't going to die soon enough for their taste without a little push.

Why make it easier for guardians to refuse food and water on behalf of persons who cannot speak for themselves? In a 1983 article, over two decades ago, reflecting on the possible outcome of this food and water debate, Daniel Callahan, then director of the prestigious Hastings Center, wrote that "...a denial of nutrition, may, in the long run, become the only effective way to make certain that a large number of biologically tenacious patients actually die." He further predicted, "Given the increasingly large pool of superannuated, chronically ill, physically marginal elderly, it could well become the *nontreatment* of choice." [Daniel Callahan, "On Feeding the Dying," *Hastings Center Report,* October 1983, p. 22.] The script was written long ago.

And please note, many people in nursing homes are on feeding tubes not because they can't eat orally, but because there are not enough staff to help them eat. One study also found that in for-profit nursing homes, African-Americans with dementia will be taken off hand feeding and put on a feeding tube sooner in the disease process than their white counterparts. Abracadabra, they're on "life support," the kind that can be removed.

One of the leaders of the end-of-life care movement, Dr. Ira Byock, was interviewed by Ragged Edge Magazine, a leading disability rights publication. He stated that Partnership for Caring and Last Acts, national leaders in the movement until they disappeared under a cloud late last year, had excluded the disability perspective, and that this exclusion was "deliberate and irresponsible." What's especially disturbing is that they had fifteen years and hundreds of millions in funding from prominent foundations, and set up surrogate decision-making protocols to end the lives of people with intellectual disabilities, without seeking the input of such individuals and the established organizations that address issues of self-determination for people who have less typical ways of receiving, processing and communicating information.

What might other disability groups have brought to the discussion table?

I recently read a journal article about the problems with advanced directives. A consistent finding in several funded studies is that people change their minds about what treatments they want, and what level of disability they will accept, as they move through the experience of having increasing disabilities. The disability community has a response to that, to use a popular phrase, "well, DUH."

And you may have seen reports of a new Alzheimer's study last year. It confirmed previous studies that caregivers have a lower opinion of their relative's quality of life with Alzheimer's than the persons themselves have, and found an explanation for the discrepancy. It seems that the caregivers project their own feelings of the burden of care-giving onto the person they care for. Once again, the disability community response is "well, DUH." And these are the very caregivers who make life-ending decisions.

And if that's not enough conflict of interest for a statutory guardian, the Kentucky Supreme Court ruled in 2004 that a public guardian may deprive life sustaining treatment from a man labeled mentally retarded, despite the financial conflict of interest for a state guardian of a ward on Medicaid.

And don't forget Professor Peter Singer, who holds an endowed chair in bioethics at Princeton, and believes that legal personhood should be subject to a cognitive test. Those who don't pass are eligible for killing if their families prefer, or for society's greater good. In fact, Arthur Caplan has repeatedly spoken about Terri Schiavo's autonomy, but I am including as an attachment to my testimony an article from the Philadelphia Inquirer in which he supports a presumption of non-treatment in ICU for people in a persistent vegetative or minimally conscious state, and limiting the information and choices provided to patients and families. This is one example of a futility policy permitting the health care provider to make the decision about treatment.

In the face of these developments, the disability rights movement has expertise to bring. But we also have an attitude about disability that diverges from the mainstream, especially the mainstream of bioethics. Frankly, I think that's why we were deliberately excluded from the last decade of policy making conducted off the public radar screen, why the right-wing-left-wing script was so important to these bioethicists, no matter how untrue and exclusionary.

Basically, the bioethicists have warped the palliative care movement into a life-ending movement. They've had hundreds of millions of dollars to work with, and they've used it to build a steamroller that's decimating the civil and constitutional rights of people in guardianship. This affects more than the disability community of today, it affects everyone, directly or through family, sooner or later. There are rules being made for who lives and who dies, but the rule-making and the medical killing are happening behind closed doors. Many things are private family matters, like parental discipline of children, for example, until they go too far. It's time to call "time out," to go back to the table and talk about how to build a health care and legal system that respects us all.

On a more practical level, what can you do to help?

MEANINGFUL FEDERAL REVIEW

Under Medicare and Medicaid law, you could provide for meaningful federal review of contested third party decisions to withhold treatment in the absence of an advance directive or personally appointed surrogate. Uphold a clear and convincing evidence standard with teeth in it. Uphold a presumption for food and fluids.

CONGRESSIONAL STUDY

Ever since the Cruzan decision in 1990, people with disabilities, old and young, have been starved and dehydrated based on surrogate or health provider decisions, but we don't know who, why, how or what factors were involved. We also know that physicians are overruling patient autonomy and denying treatment under futility policies. You could ask for all hospitals to send you their futility policies. Congressional examination of the impact of existing policies is necessary.

STATE-BY-STATE REVIEW OF LAWS AND POLICIES

Funding for a disability-rights-based state-by-state review of guardianship and health care decisions laws is needed, along with comprehensive efforts to develop reforms to safeguard against non-voluntary and involuntary euthanasia.

PUBLIC EDUCATION BY PEOPLE WITH DISABILITIES

There should be funding for public education about the perspectives of people living with significant disabilities on the difference between end-of-life decisions and decisions to end the lives of disabled people who are not otherwise dying.

OLMSTEAD IMPLEMENTATION, PASSAGE OF MICASSA
The civil rights of people with disabilities to long-term supports in the community under the U.S. Supreme Court decision in *Olmstead* should be implemented. We call for passage of the Medicaid Community Attendant Services and Supports Act, which would allow people receiving Medicaid funding to have a life in the community instead of being forced into a nursing home. This bill also includes consumer-directed options that maximize personal responsibility and reduce costs.

SUSTAIN GOVERNMENT FUNDED HEALTH CARE PROGRAMS
Conservatives who honestly supported efforts to protect the life of Terri Schiavo should work on a bipartisan basis with moderates and liberals to ensure continued appropriate funding of Medicare and Medicaid. Thank you for defeating the latest round of proposed budget cuts that threaten to result in a less-public, but very real, increase in the numbers of deaths of older and disabled people, even more prolonged and agonizing than the one experienced by Terri Schiavo, through lack of access to needed healthcare. I can't help but note that much of the power of the end-of-life movement has come from the fact that Medicare did not cover prescription drugs, including pain relievers. It was pure extortion to require people to agree to forego curative treatment in order to get pain relief, and I've been terribly disturbed to see that the new Medicare prescription drug coverage does not include pain relieving medication, continuing the pattern of extortion that forces people to accept a potentially premature death in order to receive pain relief.

To conclude, regardless of our abilities or disabilities, none of us should feel that we have to die to have dignity, that we have to die to be relieved of pain, or that we should die to stop burdening our families or society. Cognitive abilities must not be allowed to determine personhood under the laws of the United States. Reject the script you have been given by the right to die and the right to life movements. Instead, listen to the disability movement. We are your advance guard, in anticipation of the aging of our society, with decades of experience in living with disability. We want to help build a society that respects and welcomes everyone.

http://www.raggededgemagazine.com/schiavostatement.html

Issues Surrounding Terri Schindler-Schiavo Are Disability Rights Issues, Say National Disability Organizations

Oct. 27, 2003 -- We, the undersigned, come together in support of Terri Schindler-Schiavo, and her human and civil rights. We are the national spokespersons for the rights of millions of Americans with disabilities whose voices are often not heard over the din of political and religious rhetoric. We come together for those who will be touched by disability in their lifetime and who will need our help to make their voices heard.

We call on the media to join with us in ensuring that the real story about Terri Schindler-Schiavo, and thousands like her, is told.

We ask the general public, who are clearly confused about what is best for Ms. Schindler-Schiavo and others like her, to read this joint statement, signed by national organizations and our allies, and then to act accordingly to signal their support for Terri Schindler-Schiavo. Terri Schindler-Schiavo is alive. She deserves nothing less than the full advantage of human and civil rights the rest of us are fortunate to enjoy as Americans. We will not rest until her most basic humanity is secure.

The "right to life" movement has embraced her as a cause to prove "sanctity of life." The "right to die" movement believes she is too disabled to live and therefore better off dead. Yet the life-and-death issues surrounding Terri Schindler-Schiavo are first and foremost disability rights issues -- issues which affect millions of Americans with disabilities, old and young.

Can she think? Hear? Communicate? These questions apply to thousands of people with disabilities who, like Ms. Schindler-Schiavo, cannot currently articulate their views and so must rely on others as substitute decision-makers. The law requires that a guardian's decision be based on written documentation or other clear and convincing evidence of her wishes. Her husband and guardian, Michael Schiavo, says she would not have wanted to live in her current condition, but there is no written documentation or compelling evidence of this. There is just his word.

Early on in Michael Schiavo's quest to remove his wife's source of nourishment, an independent guardian was appointed upon request by Schiavo's own attorney, George Felos. That guardian, attorney Richard Pearse, issued a report to the judge stating that Michael Schiavo was not a credible witness to his wife's end-of-life wishes because he waited several years before coming forward with the claim that she wanted to die. Pearse also noted that Michael Schiavo would benefit financially from her death. Pearse was quickly removed at the request of Felos.

Experts on the issue of guardianship point out that it is always desirable that a person in Terri Schindler-Schiavo's position have an independent representative who has no particular interest in the case other than her. Since the dismissal of Pearse in 1999, Terri Schindler-Schiavo has never been appointed another independent guardian. The law Gov. Jeb Bush has just signed calls for one now.

The peculiar series of events which have led up to the current debate seem to have avoided both the judge's scrutiny and media coverage. Michael Schiavo says his wife would not have wanted to live in her current condition. And under Florida law a spouse has the right to decide, though his powers are limited by the U. S. Constitution.

Michael Schiavo conveniently remembered Terri's alleged wishes only after the malpractice judgment was awarded. A review of court records shows that of the $700,000 from a malpractice settlement Michael won that was to go for her care, over half has been spent on his legal fight to disconnect her feeding tube. Over $200,000 of it has been paid to his attorney George Felos. Michael Schiavo has refused to let his wife receive therapy from a speech pathologist, a common type of rehabilitation available to people with brain injury. A prominent expert filed an affidavit that Terri Schindler-Schiavo can swallow her own saliva, and could potentially be weaned from the feeding tube and recover some speech, so that she could indicate her own wishes.

A recent report in the New York Times Sunday Magazine stated that after months or years with little sign of consciousness, people may still be capable of complex mental activity. The reporter, Carl Zimmer, wrote, "To the medical world, ...hundreds of thousands of ...Americans who suffer from impaired consciousness present a mystery." Whether Terri Schindler-Schiavo is -- or isn't -- capable of "high level thought" is not the real issue here. It is clear that she is conscious and responsive beyond mere reflexes, as has been demonstrated by her ability to track with her eyes, respond to verbal commands by physicians who examined her on video, and react to those she loves.

She has a severe brain injury, yet has not undergone the rehabilitation that is typically given to people with this type of disability. People with severe cognitive disabilities are devalued as lives not worth living. In truth, the lives of all of us with severe disabilities are often considered expendable. This is why we are speaking out.

Americans who have disabilities -- cognitive disabilities like Ms. Schindler-Schiavo -- have rights. Congress decided that in 1990 when it passed the Americans with Disabilities Act. Yet most of society does not consider that Terri Schindler-Schiavo has any rights other than the right to die. We believe she has a right to therapy and support; we believe the Americans with Disabilities Act requires that.

Consider David Jayne, a 42 year old man with ALS. Every five seconds, a ventilator on a cart next to his bed pumps air into his lungs. He is not able to move. Twelve years ago, Jayne would have dismissed this existence as a living hell. "Yes, I am very passionate about the Terri Schindler-Schiavo issue, because I live it," says Jayne, who was profiled in TIME Magazine in 2001. Jayne, like many of us, would have once said he could not imagine living in his current state. "If someone had told me I would be paralyzed and tethered to a ventilator, yet still find meaning in life, I would not have believed them." Today he says, "It is incredibly wrong for society to decide who lives or dies based on their opinions of what level of quality of life is worth living."

In this matter of living as a disabled person, those of us who live with disability, are the experts -- not husbands, not parents, not doctors. We know that life with a disability is worth living, and we know that what makes life awful for us is the attitude of "better off dead" that drives much of the thinking surrounding people like Terri Schindler-Schiavo.

The fear of disability and the resulting bigotry adhered to by most non-disabled Americans is often cited by people with disabilities as one of the most difficult barriers to overcome. In a recent column, Bill Press stated, "I wouldn't want to live like that, would you?" We respond: "like what?" Terri Schindler-Schiavo is characterized as "...a brain-damaged woman who has been kept alive artificially." Meant to signal horror, the concept has no real meaning to us who live by "artificial" means. Is a person on dialysis being kept alive artificially? Is a person taking insulin being kept alive artificially? Is a person who undergoes open-heart surgery, or cancer treatment, or intensive care in a hospital being kept alive artificially?

It is a well-known fact among those of us who live with disabilities that a feeding tube is a low-tech support, and people who use them can and do live full and meaningful lives. It was invented in the nineteenth century and relies on nothing more than gravity to make it work.

Terri Schindler-Schiavo is said to be in a "persistent vegetative state." But is she? In court, the medical experts were divided. Fl. Circuit Judge George Greer say she has not demonstrated sufficient actions to prove "cognitive function" because her actions were not "consistent" or "reproducible." But Florida law defines "PVS" as a condition in which there is no evidence of responsiveness. By ignoring Florida law, Judge Greer has violated her due process rights, as many of us asserted in our friend-of-the court briefs.

Historically, many people with disabilities such as autism, Down syndrome and cerebral palsy have been thought to be incapable of communication. Increasingly, yesterday's assumptions about inability are being thrown out when confronted with the reality of people exceeding the low expectations put on them by others.

In 1990, the Supreme Court held, in the *Cruzan* case, that the experts' subjective determinations of things like "persistent vegetative state" invite the very "quality of life" judgments that the Court found were inappropriate.

Terri Schindler-Schiavo's fate is entwined with all disabled people who rely on surrogates. If the legal standard in cases involving termination of life support is reduced to the point where Ms. Schindler-Schiavo's "quality of life" - as determined by others - justifies her death by starvation, then what protections exist for the thousands of us who cannot speak due to disabilities?

Discrimination against people with severe disabilities is part of our nation's history. Eugenicists advocated for the involuntary euthanasia of 60,000 "hopeless cases" of persons with disabilities in institutions in the last century, and urged the killing of "defective" children. Thousands in our nation were sterilized against their will because they were "defective". Infants born with disabilities have been denied lifesaving medical treatment. And people who become severely disabled, like Terri Schindler-Schiavo, are said to be better off dead.

The need for constitutional limits on the powers of surrogate decision makers is nowhere more clear than on a question as fundamental as life or death, because the consequences of abuse or misjudgment are both ultimate and irreversible. Treating people differently based on health or disability status violates the rights of people with disabilities under the ADA. Absent proof that it is truly the person's decision, withholding medical care based on the belief that he or she would rationally want to die because of a disability is discriminatory.

Due to bias against disability and ignorance about the support systems and successful coping strategies that preserve autonomy, meaning and pleasure in life, some physicians have decided that some deaths are more rational than others and that incompetent ill and disabled people do not deserve the same type of health care that "competent" people would receive. When health care providers deny people with severe cognitive disabilities the health care they need to live, we believe they are violating the Americans with Disabilities Act.

The belief that people with disabilities like Schindler-Schiavo's are "better off dead" is longstanding but wrong. It imperils us all. As spokespeople for millions of Americans with disabilities and their families, we stand with Terri Schindler-Schiavo to protect her civil and human rights as a living American. She requires the equal protection of the law.

SIGNED:

ADA Watch
ADAPT
AIMMM - Advancing Independence
Center for Self Determination

Center on Human Policy
Citizens United Resisting Euthanasia (CURE)
Disability Rights Center
Disability Rights Education & Defense Fund
Disability Rights Project of the Public Interest Law Center of Philadelphia.
Hospice Patients Alliance
National Catholic Partnership on Disability
National Coalition for Disability Rights
National Coalition on Self-Determination
National Council on Independent Living
National Disabled Students Union
National Down Syndrome Congress
National Organization on Disability
National Spinal Cord Injury Association
Not Dead Yet
Self Advocates Becoming Empowered (SABE)
TASH
World Association of Persons with disAbilities
World Institute on Disability

http://www.notdeadyet.org/docs/equallivesUCPeditorial0405.html

Guest Opinion
All Lives Are Equal Under The Law

By Steven Eidelman, Executive Director,
The Arc of The United States, and
Stephen Drake, Research Analyst,
Not Dead Yet.

From Washington Watch: Volume 3 (2005) published by United Cerebral Palsy. Reprinted with permission.

Terri Schiavo died on April 1. Her fate was a topic of intense debate for months, and it is clear now that her death will not end the dialogue. In fact, Terri Schiavo's death may propel end-of-life issues even further into public consciousness. If there is anything positive to emerge from her ordeal, perhaps it is that more Americans will consider having the difficult end-of-life conversation with all of their loved ones.

The case of Terri Schiavo raises a number of troubling questions for Americans. For people with disabilities and their families, the case represents a "slippery slope" and raises the possibility that the right to life of people with significant intellectual and/or physical disabilities might one day be questioned.

It was just 20 years ago that many of us were enmeshed in the "Baby Doe" case when the starvation and dehydration of a newborn infant with Down Syndrome exposed this all-too-common practice in the United States. In that case, two separate judges sanctioned the death of the infant, an infant whose life could have been saved without heroics. Although few would agree with those judges' rulings today, they were fiercely defended as a protecting a private matter between families and doctors back in the mid-1980s.

Today, there are thousands of people with disabilities who use feeding tubes. For them, a feeding tube is not life support or heroic intervention, but the normal way they get food and water. When they are hospitalized for any reason -- however minor -- they risk having their normal means of eating and drinking being classified as "extraordinary treatment" or "life support."

Few of us have enough experience with severe disability to make an informed choice in an advance directive, but clearly, having a significant disability does not mean you are "pre-dead." People with disabilities agree with the Americans with

Disabilities Act -- that "disability is a natural part of the human experience." Indeed, so is death.

The persistent vegetative state diagnosis is another matter, however, one fraught with unreliability. The fair and just allocation of health care and long term support resources is often in the back of our minds, whether we talk about it or not. These are ample reasons why we must put aside the partisan posturing and have an open and inclusive discussion of the issues at hand.

The disability community today is troubled by the possibility that Terri Schiavo's life -- and death -- may cause legal protections for people who have guardians to be dismantled, making it easier for guardians to kill by withholding food and water. There must be a way to balance a person's right to expressly refuse treatment against a person's right not to be deprived of life without due process of law. Due process of law must appreciate the wishes and interests of people with disabilities, even if their lives are devalued by other people. Today, we fear that is not the case.

Terri Schiavo's wishes were not documented, and her husband and family had many conflicts. Advocates for people with disabilities would never have wished to deprive Terri Schiavo of her right to self-determination regarding the end of her life, had her wishes been documented in a living will and/or power of attorney. But they were not.

Given these ambiguities, the disability community feels that the courts should have ruled on the side of sustaining her life, not allowing her to die. The disability community, from many years of grappling with these issues, feels that in such cases, it is best to assume that life is preferable over death. This is the position of 26 national disability groups, many of which represent people like Terri Schiavo who have guardians.

State laws governing surrogate decision-making vary and are often the result of well-funded advocacy from a narrow group of professionals, not involving the viewpoint of people with disabilities. When a guardian is needed -- particularly a state-appointed guardian -- the possibility for conflicts of interest is clear. Thus, the Schiavo case has focused attention on the need for a "federal floor" to protect people under guardianship. Research indicates that people with living wills and advance directives frequently change their minds when the time comes to implement those directives. Once people experience severe disability, their sense of horror about disability usually fades. We also know that people who "cannot speak for themselves" are often able to use assistive technologies that allow them to communicate their wishes, hopes, fears, and good-byes even if they can no longer speak. In today's climate, it might be even more important to write down what you do want than what you do not want.

In addition, we must, as a society, stop using the term "persistent vegetative state." Too many people with significant disabilities have been called "vegetables," and this needs to stop. It is beyond demeaning. It is dehumanizing. In fact, some of the people who use the term most freely are doctors, and what often comes next is a discussion of the death or warehousing of the individual with such a pejorative label.

For a person with serious disabilities, the debate should not be about whether or not they are going to "get better" some day. Disability is a fact of life, every day of our lives. Millions of Americans are disabled, and for millions more, it is just a matter of time. None of us is guaranteed an able body or mind for life.

People with disabilities sometimes have wonderful lives, and sometimes they have lousy lives. They are just like other Americans. Just because a person has a significant disability does not mean that he or she does not love life. It does not mean that they should be assumed to be better off dead.

It is time for a call to conscience to both the Right and the Left. Guardianship should not be a death ship. People like Terri Schiavo, people with disabilities, are persons under the law, and they deserve constitutional protection.

The disability community is grateful that so many in Congress stepped up to support Terri Schiavo's right to live, even though we are concerned about the precedent that was established. We would like to see Congress follow up with the same level of concern in making sure we can provide care and support for the millions of Americans with disabilities by supporting Medicaid Community Attendant Services and Supports Act, legislation that would allow thousands of adults with disabilities who have Medicaid funded services to have a life in their communities, not just stay to alive in an institution. We call on the Congress to ensure continued support for Medicaid and other programs people need; and we look forward to the passage of the Family Opportunity Act, to allow families of children with significant disabilities to buy into the Medicaid program in order to help their sons and daughters live at home in the community, rather than being banished to a nursing home or institution.

Terri Schiavo's case is every family's nightmare. But disability doesn't have to be a nightmare. Even if our nation disagrees on how we define compassion, we must certainly agree that all lives are equal under the law.

http://www.philly.com/mld/inquirer/4437797.htm
Posted on Mon, Nov. 04, 2002 <

Penn hospital to limit its care in futile cases

Severely brain-damaged patients won't get certain treatments, as a rule.

By Stacey Burling

Inquirer Staff Writer

The Hospital of the University of Pennsylvania is taking another crack at one of medicine's thorniest issues: how to treat people who have no hope of recovery.

The hospital's ethics committee has approved unusual new guidelines that include limits on high-tech treatment for patients with severe brain damage.

Under the guidelines, intensive care would not routinely be given to patients in a persistent vegetative or minimally conscious state. Only patients who had explicitly requested such care would get it.

The guidelines, which will not be implemented for at least a year, also say what the hospital will do for patients, both when there is hope for recovery and, later, when the goal shifts to providing good "hygiene, preservation of dignity, and alleviation of discomfort or suffering."

The rules are meant to define good care, just as the hospital does for conditions such as asthma or diabetes.

"Over the last 20 to 30 years, medicine has evolved a notion that limits are taboo, that whatever patients want or demand, they have every right to expect," said Horace DeLisser, a pulmonary and critical-care doctor who also cochairs the ethics committee. "What we're saying is that we think that care is not simply about giving more machines, that care has to be tailored to these patients."

Communication with families about patient prognosis and treatment will remain an important part of care, he said, and an assertive family could probably successfully fight the new policy. Penn also has a conflict-resolution process and offers the option of transferring the patient to another hospital.

About a quarter of deaths now occur in intensive-care units, said Robert Truog, professor of anesthesia and medical ethics at Harvard Medical School. More than half of those occur after withdrawal of life-sustaining treatment.

Although more than 90 percent of people say in surveys that they would not want to be kept alive in a vegetative state, less than a quarter make it clear in advance when they would want doctors to give up, said Robert Perkel, chairman of the ethics committee at Thomas Jefferson University Hospital.

Wesley J. Smith, a California lawyer and author of The Culture of Death: The Assault on Medical Ethics in America , is a longtime critic of hospital policies that limit care when doctors think patients lack sufficient quality of life. This approach is dangerous because it "creates a hierarchy of human worth," he said. "What is going on here is a statement that certain lives have less value than other lives, and that the values of the institution trump those of the patient."

Doctors who work in ICUs say they are sometimes asked to perform grotesque procedures on people who are capable of feeling little more than pain. CPR can break bones. It is almost impossible to insert certain types of intravenous lines in bodies twisted by a long period of brain damage, DeLisser said. "It approaches assault. You're really just attacking these patients."

Doctors and nurses go home after treating such patients feeling not only that they have done no good, but that they have caused pain, only to delay an inevitable death.

Under the new Penn guidelines, DeLisser said, if a patient in a persistent vegetative state - a step above coma - were transferred to the Hospital of the University of Pennsylvania with a fever, he would get the sorts of treatments he could receive as an outpatient: blood tests, antibiotics, a chest X-ray, urine tests. He might be admitted to a general medical bed. But, in the absence of an advance directive from the patient, he would not be admitted to an ICU. He would not be put on a ventilator or breathing machine. (If he were already on a ventilator, the hospital would not take him off.) He would not get surgery.

Doctors at HUP now use a hodgepodge of approaches, DeLisser said, but "for the most part... the unwritten approach is actually what we've written in the guidelines."

At Penn, there are one or two intractable conflicts each year, said John Hansen-Flaschen, chief of Penn's pulmonary, allergy and critical care division. The most recent involved an elderly woman with many medical problems. She suffered a serious stroke after refusing amputation of a leg. The woman had been "rescued over and over again," but she was "dying from the outside in," Hansen-Flaschen said. Both legs had gangrene; she had large bed sores. "Portions of her body looked like a cadaver pulled out of a grave," he said. The family would not sign a do-not-resuscitate order. She eventually died after a failed resuscitation attempt.

Hospitals have wrestled with the controversial concept of medical futility for more than a decade. Many have decided that it is futile to try to define futility. A growing number have opted for creating a procedure for dealing with conflicts about withholding or withdrawing care, an approach the American Medical Association has endorsed. Massachusetts General Hospital, Children's Hospital of Boston, and, in this area, three hospitals in the Mercy Health System have developed such procedures. In Texas, hospital conflict-resolution procedures are now backed up by a state law.

But Lawrence Schneiderman, a medical ethicist at the University of California San Diego, says hospitals also need to define when that process is justified, as many California hospitals do. Most judge appropriateness of treatment on the basis of patient awareness and potential for appreciating the care.

Penn's guidelines, and another set of rules it has governing withholding or withdrawal of life support, do not use the word "futility." They do say, "The purpose of intensive life support is to sustain or restore a meaningful survival for the patient, where meaningful refers to a survival that can be valued and appreciated by the patient."

The weak point of virtually all policies is that hospital leaders fear they would lose a lawsuit if they denied care demanded by a family. They will rarely back doctors all the way, so there's little case law on the subject.

Cathy Mikus, associate counsel for the Mercy system, said that in the year since its policy went into effect, all disputes have been resolved. She is confident the hospital would support its staff if agreement could not be reached. "If we have to go all the way through this process," she said, "we have physicians who feel very, very strongly that the care is not appropriate under the circumstances."

Etienne Phipps, director of the medical ethics program at Albert Einstein Medical Center, doubts her hospital could successfully fight a family in "this current legal environment." She also doubts it would want to. It is "highly likely" the administration would side with the family, she said, "because of the values of the hospital toward supporting the patient and family values over everything."

The issue of when to limit care arose in the 1970s, after it became clear that life-sustaining treatments such as mechanical ventilation can sometimes be "more burdensome than beneficial," said Eric Krakauer, associate director of the palliative care service at Mass General.

Back in those days, however, doctors were the ones more likely to want to "do everything," and families of patients such as Karen Ann Quinlan were asking to pull back. At the same time, the patient empowerment movement was gaining steam, and doctors began paying more attention to patient and family wishes in medical decisions.

By the early 1990s, many doctors began to worry that some dying patients were getting too much care. Patients and their families, concerned that HMOs and money-conscious hospitals were trying to cut costs, were getting less trusting. Now, conflicts are more likely to be between families who want more and doctors who want less.

Arthur Caplan, director of Penn's Center for Bioethics, said doctors have compounded the problem by offering families a menu of choices.

"That's not the best way to approach the family," Caplan said, "because it makes the family feel responsible for ending the life of their loved one."

It's better to say, "In our best judgment, sadly, there's nothing more we can do. We're going to begin the process of stopping aggressive care."

Doctors could also head off disagreements by explaining life support better on the front end. "You should never start an intervention, a feeding tube, dialysis, where you haven't had a little bit of discussion about when you're going to stop it," Caplan said.

DeLisser says it's vital to define the type of care patients will get, no matter what, because families often fear the hospital will stop taking care of their loved one if they agree to limit life support. "Medicine, I don't think, has recognized that what patients and their families really want is... they don't want to be abandoned."

Contact Stacey Burling at 215-854-4944 or sburling@phillynews.com.

Mr. SOUDER. Thank you very much for your testimony. All of the witnesses' full statements will be included in the record.

Our next witness, Bob Sedlmeyer is from my hometown of Fort Wayne, IN. He and his wife Cheryl, and I know he will tell us some of the story, but I want to say to those, in addition to those in the room, to those who are watching on television, Members or staff, the media, we can argue about what our Government policy should be, but Bob and Cheryl have practiced what parents who have loved their kids and have watched their lives be impacted for I think 19 years now, somewhere in that amount, of where they can go on vacation, what they can do, how much money they are going to have, they are not a rich family, they are a hardworking family, and yet they made keeping and feeding their daughter a center of their lives and really appreciate that example of love, regardless of what government does. And so we are looking forward to hearing your testimony.

STATEMENT OF BOB SEDLMEYER

Mr. SEDLMEYER. Thank you for that affirmation, Chairman Souder. Good afternoon. I play many roles in life. I am a teacher, consultant, youth minister, son, and husband. I speak to you today, however, as a father, the father of Pam, Rob, Valerie, Vanessa, and Tim.

Let me begin by telling you about my daughter, Valerie. Valerie is 19 years old. Her name comes from the Latin word for "strength," but if she were by my side today you would think that she is one of the weakest persons you have ever seen. Valerie suffers from a congenital defect of her circulatory system called an AV malformation. It is a condition that results in a knot of blood vessels instead of an orderly array of arteries and veins. Her knot was formed deep inside her brain. From the moment she was born her brain was starved for oxygen. A series of experimental surgeries saved her life but could not prevent the extensive and permanent damage to her brain.

Valerie is not unlike Terri Schiavo. Spinal fluid fills the areas where her brain has withered and died. Some would say that she is in a persistent vegetative state. She cannot speak. What she sees and hears is a mystery. Her fingers curl tightly into her palms. She has metal rods in her back and right leg to support her fragile bones. She must be carried or carted everywhere. She has been fed through a tube three times a day for the past 17 years. She is given medication to control her seizures and to relax her ever-tense muscles. Her care has cost many thousands of dollars, a financial burden that has been carried in large part by insurance, Medicaid, and the generosity of those physicians who have attended her.

Valerie's prognosis is not hopeful. She will never gain more awareness of herself nor the world around her. When she was 2 months old and well enough to be released from the hospital, her mother and I were invited to an exit conference with the attending neurologist. He was blunt, and his words will forever be etched into my memory. "Everything from the ears up is gone," he said. "I recommend that you place her into an institution." We took her home instead.

Caring for Valerie has never been easy, but it has become routine. A typical day for her begins at 5:30 a.m. Her mother wakes her up, dresses her, feeds her, and places her into a wheelchair. A bus picks her up and takes her to the local high school where she joins five other students in the special needs classroom. She is given occupational and physical therapy and is taken on occasional field trips. She receives abundant attention from teachers, aides, and her fellow classmates. One boy even calls Valerie his girlfriend.

When she comes home, we place her on a cot in the family room. Sometimes, when the weather is nice, we take her for a walk or just let her sit in the warm sunshine. About 8 p.m., after she is fed and diapered, we carry her to bed.

Besides the excellent educational services Valerie receives, we are also grateful for other services for which she qualifies through the Medicaid waiver program. A therapist visits her once a week in our home, and a caseworker tracks her well-being quarterly. She also receives several hours a month of respite care. This has given us welcome breaks from the intense physical and emotional stress of caring for her, and afforded our family opportunities to take much-needed vacations. This program also pays for her food and diapers. And since she turned 18, Valerie receives SSI. These funds supplement our household income to provide for her clothing, transportation, medical, and assistive device needs.

Valerie will ever remain in need of total care. She will never hold a job. She will never vote in an election. She will never exercise her freedoms of speech, assembly, or religion. She will never make a positive contribution to society. Of what value, then, is her life? For what purpose, then, should her life be sustained?

I am not a philosopher, I am not a theologian, I am not a physician or a judge. I claim no special knowledge. I am a father. And I am a man of simple faith. I have had to wrestle with these questions for many years. I know that my answers will find little favor with current polls and pundits. I believe the merits of Valerie's life cannot be determined by how she can think or what she can do. I believe her worth cannot be evaluated by how much she is wanted either by me or anyone else. I believe that her value cannot be judged by the ones who may see her as less than fully human, but only by the One who sees her as made in His image and likeness. And it is only through the eyes of faith that I have come to see her in that way, too.

I have come to realize that her life, as wounded and powerless as it is, is not a burden to bear but a gift to cherish. It is not something over which to exert control but to assume stewardship. I began to see that her long-suffering has a purpose. She has taught me how to love unconditionally, how to give sacrificially, and how to serve humbly. She has made me a better husband and father. I will forever be grateful to the many doctors, nurses, social workers, therapists, teachers, clergy, family, and friends who have also seen the value of her life.

Many have concurred with the sentiment that they would not want to live like that. Many have asserted that Terri Schiavo had a right to die. It is frightening to me that the value of Ms. Schiavo's life, as measured by the scales of our justice system, did not merit even food and water. I fervently hope that such scales will never be used to assess the value of my daughter's life, and dreadfully anticipate the day when her right to die may become her duty to die.

So I appeal to this subcommittee to promote policies and pass legislation that both protects the lives of incapacitated citizens like my daughter and encourages and enables their families to provide for their needs. Thank you again for the opportunity to testify on these matters, and may you be guided by wisdom and compassion as you consider your recommendations.

[The prepared statement of Mr. Sedlmeyer follows:]

Testimony by Bob Sedlmeyer
Subcommittee on Criminal Justice, Drug Policy and Human Resources
Hearing on Federal Health Programs and Those Who Cannot Care for Themselves: What Are Their Rights and Our Responsibilities
April 19, 2005

Good afternoon. My name is Bob Sedlmeyer. I appreciate this opportunity to share my experiences of caring for an incapacitated child. I am an Associate Professor of Computer Science at Indiana University Purdue University Fort Wayne. I am a consultant to Raytheon Net Centric Systems. I am a lay minister for the LifeTeen youth program at St. Vincent de Paul Catholic Church. I am son to Bob and Mary Lou and husband to Cheryl. I speak to you today, however, as the father of Pam, Rob, Valerie, Vanessa, and Tim.

Let me begin by telling you about my daughter, Valerie. Valerie is 19 years old. Her name comes from the Latin word for "strength," but if she were by my side today you would think that she is one of the weakest persons you have ever seen. Valerie suffered a congenital defect of her circulatory system called an AV-malformation. It is a condition that results in a knot of blood vessels instead of an orderly array of arteries and veins. Her knot was formed deep inside her brain. From the moment she was born her brain was starved for oxygen. A series of experimental surgeries saved her life but could not prevent the extensive and permanent damage to her brain.

Valerie is not unlike Terri Schiavo. Spinal fluid fills the areas where her brain has withered and died. Some would say that she is in a persistent vegetative state. She cannot speak. What she sees and hears is a mystery. Her fingers curl tightly into her palms. She has metal rods in her back and right leg to support her fragile bones. She must be carried or carted everywhere. She has been fed through a tube three times a day for the past seventeen years. She is given medication to control her seizures and relax her ever- tense muscles. Her care has cost many thousands of dollars, a financial burden that has been carried in large part by insurance, Medicaid, and the generosity of those physicians who have attended her.

Valerie's prognosis is not hopeful. She will never gain more awareness of herself nor the world around her. When she was two months old and well enough to be released from the hospital, her mother and I were invited to an exit conference with the attending neurologist. He was blunt, and his words will forever be etched into my memory. "Everything from the ears up is gone," he said. "I'd recommend that you place her into an institution." We took her home instead.

Caring for Valerie has never been easy, but it has become routine. A typical day for her begins at 5:30 am. Her mother wakes her up, dresses her, feeds her and places her into her wheelchair. A bus picks her up and takes her to the local high school where she joins five other students in the special needs classroom. She is given occupational and physical therapy and is taken on occasional field trips. She receives abundant attention from teachers, aides and her fellow classmates. One boy even calls Valerie his girlfriend.

When she comes home we place her on a cot in the family room. Sometimes, when the weather is nice, we take her for a walk or just let her sit in the warm sunshine. About 8 pm, after she is fed and diapered we carry her to bed.

Besides the excellent educational services that Valerie receives, we are also grateful for other services for which she qualifies through the Medicaid Waiver program. A therapist visits her once a week in our home, and a caseworker tracks her well-being quarterly. She also receives several hours a month of respite care. This has given us welcome breaks from the intense physical and emotional stress of caring for her, and afforded our family opportunities to take much-needed vacations. This program also pays for her food and diapers. Since she turned 18, Valerie has also received Supplemental Social Security Income. These funds supplement our household income to provide for her clothing, transportation, medical, and assistive device needs.

Valerie will ever remain a life in need of total care. She will never hold a job. She will never vote in an election. She will never exercise her freedoms of speech, assembly or religion. She will never make a positive contribution to society. Of what value, then, is her life? For what purpose, then, should her life be sustained?

I am not a philosopher, theologian, physician or judge. I claim no special knowledge. I am a father. I have a simple faith. I have had to wrestle with these questions for many years. I know that my answers will find little favor with current polls and pundits. The merits of Valerie's life cannot be determined by how she can think or what she can do. Her worth cannot be evaluated by how much she is wanted by me or anyone else. Her value cannot be judged by the ones who may see her as less than fully human, but only by the One who sees her as made in His image and likeness. And it is only through the eyes of faith that I have come to see her in that way, too.

I have come to realize that her life, as wounded and powerless as it is, is not a burden to bear but a gift to cherish. It is not something over which to exert control but to assume stewardship. I began to see that her long-suffering has a purpose. She has taught me how to love unconditionally, how to give sacrificially, and how to serve humbly. She has made me a better husband and father. I will forever be grateful to the many doctors, nurses, social workers, therapists, teachers, clergy, family and friends who have also seen the value of her life.

Many have concurred with the sentiment that they would not want to live "like that".
Many have asserted that Terri Schiavo had a right to die. It is frightening to me that the value of Ms. Schiavo's life, as measured by the scales of our justice system, did not merit even food and water. I fervently hope that such scales will never be used to assess the value of my daughter's life, and dreadfully anticipate the day when her right to die may become her duty to die.

I appeal to this subcommittee to promote policies and legislation that both protects the lives of incapacitated citizens like my daughter and encourages and enables their families to provide for their needs. Thank-you again for the opportunity to testify on these matters, and may you be guided by wisdom and compassion as you consider your recommendations.

Mr. SOUDER. Thank you.

Our next witness is Kate Adamson, from Redondo Beach, CA.

STATEMENT OF KATE ADAMSON

Ms. ADAMSON. My name is Kate Adamson. The left side of my body is partially paralyzed. I was once completely and totally paralyzed; I could not move at all, I could not even blink my eyes. Yet, I was completely conscious and aware and I was able to feel pain. I just could not tell anyone about it. I know what it is like to be hooked up to respirators, to be fed by a feeding tube, I know what it is like to have your feeding tube turned off for 8 days. Today, you will hear my opinion and hear about my personal experience and unique perspective on the question before this committee.

One night I was fit and healthy, a 33 year-old mother of two small toddlers with everything to live for, and the next morning I was totally paralyzed. According to the doctors, I had less than one chance in a million to survive. Ten years ago, before this happened to me, I thought I was pretty clear about what I would want if I ever suffered a catastrophic injury or illness. I was sure that I would rather die than be a burden to anyone. I wanted no heroic measures taken when my time came. Of course, I never expected my time to come soon. But for me it came at 33. And as I hung onto life, for dear life, I realized how little we know about things until we have been there ourselves.

We do not know it will be like, or what we will want until it happens to us. When I found myself in that condition, I knew that I wanted to live. And as I lay in the hospital bed listening to the doctors talk about my impending death and their plans not to treat me, I can assure you that my idea of the right thing to do for an incapacitated person had drastically changed.

Let me tell you what it was like to be aware of what is going on but to have to rely on others to speak for you. When they inserted a feeding tube into my stomach, thinking I could not feel, in fact, I could feel everything but I could do nothing. I felt everything they were doing. I felt every cut, every second. And I had no way to communicate. I was totally locked into my body, unable to speak, unable to move a muscle. And at one point my tube was turned off for 8 days and I suffered all the pains and agonies of starvation. I was in excruciating pain, in silence. I was on the inside screaming out: I do not want to die. Do not starve me. I want to live. Please feed me something.

Now if you asked me today if it was worth going through everything I went through to live, I would say without doubt, without a hesitation, yes. As a disabled person, my life is as important as any life. My children love me as much as any children love their parents, my husband loves me as much as when I had the use of two good arms and two good legs.

When I waged my fight to get treatment, the way life was viewed in this country was a potent weapon in my husband's fight to save me. It would not be so today. In 1995, you did not do your best to speed up death. You did not starve people to death assuming that it would be a painless death. Today people do. Today, courts back up selfish disregard for human life with court orders that terminate life. The courts do not even require evidence proving the issues of life and death beyond a reasonable doubt. You can take a life is the person's life is deemed by so-called experts to be not worth living. Courts are even willing to end lives based upon flimsy hearsay evidence presented by guardians who may no longer have their ward's best interests at heart or may even have a conflict of interest.

In this country, in the year 2005, Federal judges and State judges said to people like me that we do not count. A judge said to my family that I was not worth as much as an able-bodied person. You think I am wrong? Then tell me of one case when this Congress or any courts of this land would allow you to starve to death an able-bodied male or female. Yet, that is just what was done in the Terri Schiavo case. If I am wrong, then explain it to me or to the other millions of disabled people in America, who, I might add, vote.

No person should be put to death in this country again without providing that person the same rights you afford to mass murders. Michael Schiavo had the right to hire all the experts he wanted, and he had the money to do it using the $1.3 million he received in the malpractice case. Unbelievably, he was able to hire attorneys and experts who are proponents of euthanasia using the very money that was supposed to be used to treat and try to rehabilitate Terri. Scott Petersen, at the people's expense, got all the experts he needed to defend his life. But faced with the prospect of having a judge end her life, Terri Schiavo initially had no experts to speak for her and had no attorney to speak in her favor for her life, and she could not even use the funds recovered in the malpractice case for her to get the help she needed in the legal system. There is no balance of fairness afforded to her.

So here comes my opinion. Never again allow judges the sole discretion to make these kinds of decisions without affording the condemned all the rights of a criminal accused. Give the courts clear direction forcing them to make the guardian prove every element of a case that would result in taking a human life, no matter what condition that human life is in, beyond a reasonable doubt. Never allow simple hearsay evidence on any matter that would take a life. Make it mandatory for every disabled person to have a lawyer whose sole job is to argue for his or her life with the presumption in the favor of life. And in all such cases pay for that lawyer if the person cannot afford it. Provide that lawyer with all the tools he or she would have if they were defending a mass murder.

We are not asking for special rights. Disabled people do not want to be treated as special human beings. They just want to be treated as human beings. Thank you.

[The prepared statement of Ms. Adamson follows:]

WRITTEN STATEMENT OF KATE ADAMSON

April 19, 2005

United States House of Representatives

Committee on Government Reform

Subcommittee on Criminal Justice, Drug Policy and Human Resources

"Federal Health Programs and Those Who Cannot Care for Themselves: What Are Their Rights, and Our Responsibilities?"

My name is Kate Adamson. I'm a hemiplegic; the left side of my body is paralyzed. I can talk to you about the issues of care for incapacitated adults as very few people can. I know what life sustaining measures are like from first hand experience. I know what it is like to be hooked up to respirators, to be fed by a feeding tube. I even know what it is like to have your feeding tube turned off for eight days. You will hear in these hearings from many people who have opinions, but in my case you will hear not only my opinion but you will hear about my first hand experience.

10 years ago I had some very firm ideas about the kind of medical care I would want if I ever suffered a catastrophic injury or illness. I knew in my mind that I never wanted to be a burden to my family. I knew that I would be brave and that I could face death as a modern person. I wanted no heroics when my time came. Of course my idea of when my time would come was pushed off to somewhere in the mid 21 first century, when at 96, I would have my 36 great grand children at my side.

I imagine that the honorable members of this committee all have very strong ideas themselves about what they would want to do. Well here - the first thing I can tell you about my personal experience: forget your notions. My time came a little bit short of 96; at 33 I faced death. I was as fit as a person could be and as healthy as a person could ever be. So, if anyone thinks it can't happen to them, they are surely wrong. At 33 I was a young mother with everything to live for and the next moment a totally helpless person who could do nothing for herself. I was now a woman hooked up to every machine imaginable with four IVs running into my arms and a tube placed into my stomach providing me the only nourishment I was able to receive. I was a woman who, outwardly, appeared to have suffered such a catastrophic injury that surely she would die soon. I was a woman who was fully conscious, alert, awake, aware and in extreme pain with no capability of expressing what I thought.

As I laid there in my room I heard the doctors talk about my impending death and their plans not to treat me. I can assure you at that moment of abject fear and despair my idea of what was the right thing to do for an incapacitated person had drastically changed from my early uneducated beliefs. You may think you know what you will do when you are in a fox hole, but you don't. If you have not been there, you should not presume to know how that person really feels.

If I had not had a loving determined husband to speak for me, I would be dead now. I think if I had not known I could count on my husband Steven to do everything he could to save me, I might have given up at the beginning of this episode and died. Of course, knowing what I know now, I realize that my death would have been agonizingly slow and painful.

When I waged my fight to get treatment, the way life was viewed in this county was a potent weapon in my husband's fight to save me. In 1995 you just didn't let people die without a fight. You just didn't starve people to death. Today we do. Today courts back up foolishness and selfish disregard for human life with court orders that terminate life solely because some judge determines that that life is not worth living. Just because someone is a judge, they are given the unbridled power and authority to inject their own, perhaps misguided, opinions regarding the so-called value of a human life.

Judges are willing to end lives based upon the shakiest of pure hearsay evidence, often evidence presented by guardians who may no longer have their wards best interests at heart or, as Judge Greer found with Michael Schiavo, guardians who have a conflict of interest. A husband who may no longer love his wife, a spouse who has moved on and formed another primary relationship are allowed to provide hearsay evidence in support of their conflicted interest, evidence that has the power to snuff out human life. They are supported by people like Dr. Ronald Cranford, who is touted as an expert in this field, who has expressed the opinion that it is near barbaric to care for some people who are disabled just because he thinks there is no value to living life with a significant disability.

I doubt I would have been asked to testify today if not for what happened to Terri Schiavo. I think the Schiavo case is a awful blot on this country that will stain us for years and years to come. I believe that Michael Schiavo lied about what Terri said. I might be wrong about that or I maybe right. It is so hard to tell who was telling the truth about what Terri wanted. What is for sure though is just how easy it is to put whatever words you want into the mouths of those who cannot speak for themselves. We should learn from the Schiavo case and never again allow any court to trust the kind of flimsy evidence that was used to put Terri Schiavo to death. We should never again allow such a decision to be made by one single judge, whose judgment may be right or may be wrong. We should never again allow courts to ignore new scientific capabilities or evidence where a human life is involved.

Even if Terri said the things Michael said she did, it should not have been enough to warrant taking her life. Terri was 22 when she was supposed to have stated her dying wishes; she had no way of really knowing what the true import of her words could be. She had no idea at that age just how precious life was. I am not sure anyone can tell what a gift life is until they actually face losing it. One only need look at the number of people who have been exonerated of involvement in a crime since the ability to analyze DNA was established a few years ago. Many of those people actually were released from death row. Terri Schiavo should have been given the chance to gain her release from the death row imposed upon her by her estranged husband, a misguided judge and lawyers and so-called experts who are, in fact, proponents of euthanasia.

If you asked me prior to my stroke if I wanted to live in my present condition if I wanted to go through what I went through just to live, I think that I likely would have said no. If you ask me today if I want to live as I am or if I think it was worth going through all I went through to live, the answer would be a resounding YES!

I am disabled and I accept it. As a disabled person I can tell you something special about how precious life is. My life is as important as any life. My children love me as much as any children love their parents; my husband loves me as much as when I had two good arms and two good legs. I have an active life; I work, I spend money and I vote. Should I have less right to medical care than the members of this committee? Should I or any other disabled person be made to feel like a second class citizen? Tha is exactly how I feel today.

Why wouldn't I feel second class? Judges in this year 2005, both Federal and State, have clearly said to people like me that we don't count. Judges said to my family that I was not worth as much as an able bodied person. You think I am wrong? Then tell me one case when this Congress or the courts of this land have ever allowed an able bodied man or women to starve to death. Please explain to my children how starving Terri Schiavo was any different than taking a life in the gas chamber, aside from the fact that the gas chamber is less excruciatingly painful, and does not take as long to kill someone.

I know you won't like me saying this, but they did start with the disabled in Nazi Germany. If you start allowing judges who are accountable to no one to make decisions about what lives are worth protecting and what lives are not worth protecting you are farther along to acting like Nazi Germany than you may realize. First kill the conscience of the people and then you can kill the people.

Terri's case went so badly array because antiquated civil guardianship law was applied to a life or death question. No person should ever be put to death in this country again without providing that person with the same rights you afford to mass murderers.

Michael Schiavo, having won 1.3 million dollars in a malpractice case, from a court he asked to give him the power to care for his wife for the next 50 years, had all the money he needed to hire the experts he needed to "prove" his wife was nothing more than a carrot. They once thought I was carrot too and I can tell you that you can always find so-called experts to say anything. Every member of this committee who is an attorney knows just how right I am about this.

Scott Petersen at the peoples cost got all the experts he needed to defend his life. Terri Schiavo a poor innocent woman got not one penny to help her defend her life. Michael was a selfish misguided man, but he did not take Terri's life, the courts of this country took Terri's life. The order directing the removal of Terri's tube was signed by a judge, not by Michael Schiavo. WE THE PEOPLE took Terri's life. The blood of it is on all our hands. Yours and mine.

If you are looking to make things better in the future, not merely to mourn for Terri Schiavo, then there are some things I believe that you can do that will help. Here comes my opinion.

Never again allow judges the sole discretion to make these kinds of decisions. The courts are no more up to playing God than the legislature or executive is; but if you, our representatives in Congress, did the kind of things the courts have done in the Schiavo case, at least we, the people, could vote you out of office. In many cases no one can remove a judge from office even though that judge acts with blatant bias, favoritism or simply an unreasonable insistence upon not ever admitting the possibility of having made a mistake. With such power, there must at least be some means whereby decisions of judges, which may be wrong or improper, can be corrected. That would require that appellate courts establish different tests to apply to the review of such decisions. One of the significant hallmarks of our judicial system was the right to a trial by a jury yet we are so cavalier about denying that for the sake of expedience. We are so loathe to overturn the decision of a trial judge, again, for the sake of expedience. Expedience in the courts should ALWAYS take a back seat to fairness and justice.

I am saying that this Congress needs to take back its rightful role as the final authority on the proper role of the judiciary. Proper checks and balances among the three branches of government do not dictate that we must have a completely unfettered judiciary. The role of Congress should, properly, be to make sure that courts dispense not only "justice" but that the justice meted out by the courts is fair.

All the power government has in this country is on loan from its people. That is what makes America great. If we forget were we came from and who we are than this noble experiment in government is over.

I have lost my confidence in judges alone to make these kinds of life and death decisions. I, for one, want my legislators to better control the judges who are given the task of deciding life and death. I want to require a guardian who wants to end a life to prove every element of his or her case, no mater what the condition of that human life, beyond a reasonable doubt. More than a cursory review of that trial court level decision must be available – particularly for those who are unable to speak for themselves, those who are sometimes the weakest among us. I want you to see to it that every person has a right to have a lawyer whose sole job is to fight for and to argue for their life to be preserved, making that mandatory in all such cases and to pay for that lawyer if the person can not afford it. I want to see to it that the lawyer has all the tools he or she would have if they were defending the worst mass murderer. I want you to make sure that, in a hearing on matters like Terri Schiavo's, the so-called playing field is level, that the presumption, in the absence of express and explicit written documentation to the contrary from the patient, that the presumption ALWAYS favors life. I want you to see to it that monies recovered for the benefit of someone like Terri can never again be put to use to kill her instead of being used for the intended purpose as it was expressed when it was awarded. I want you to see to it that, in a disputed case like Terri Schiavo's, when a spouse abandons the marriage by living with someone else as though married, or by having children outside of that marriage, that they forfeit the right to keep acting like they are still the spouse.

Mr. SOUDER. Thank you very much for your testimony.

We will now close with Mr. Robert Destro, professor at Columbus School of Law, The Catholic University of America. And you really did not have to have an accident to try to testify today. [Laughter.]

STATEMENT OF ROBERT DESTRO

Mr. DESTRO. Thank you, Mr. Chairman. I do apologize for not getting a statement in to you. But as you can see, I am living proof of the adage that anyone can become disabled at the blink of an eye. And mine was, unfortunately, at the blink of a Washington flyer taxicab that rear-ended my car last week. So I did not get a chance to finish it. With your permission, I will submit the written comments for the record.

I appear today not only as a civil rights advocate who specializes in discrimination on the basis of disability and religion, I was privileged to serve as counsel for both Governor Bush and the Schindler family in the Schiavo case. And if I can underscore anything in my testimony today, it would really be that I really do not think, based on my experience certainly as a member of the Civil Rights Commission back in the 1980's, as well as in my experience throughout the Schiavo case, that either the courts or the media really understand the issue of discrimination against people with disabilities, especially those involving disabilities caused by a brain injury or a disease.

I think that it is kind of the ultimate when you listen to the discussion of people on CNN and Fox News and MSNBC, you can almost hear the, "Well I really would not want to live that way if that were me." But it is not them, and it is not the job of the lawyers or the doctors or the guardians or the judges to project their feelings on someone with a disability.

As my colleagues on the panel have pointed out, and in far better terms than I could ever do, the reality of what a person with a disability experiences is known to them and can be experienced. And as one of the commentators on Fox News pointed out to me when I told him that really our goal in the Schiavo case, after Congress passed the law, was to get the case in front of a jury, and he was a little bit surprised about that because he assumed, like many people did, that this was just a bunch of crazy pro-lifers who were out to keep somebody who really wanted to die alive. But the fact of the matter is that Judge Greer himself abrogated Florida law when he found that Terri was partially cognizant of things and that, as a matter of fact, under Florida law she was not in a persistent vegetative state. And he was quite shocked. He said, "Do you really want to go to a jury? Why?" And the answer is, "Well, we really do need to know what her condition is."

Before we start making distinctions and make determinations that can never be reversed, we need to know what is the actual condition of the patient. We would expect that in an informed consent proceeding for a person who does not have any disabilities but who is about to undergo some kind of corrective or even cosmetic surgery. And there is no excuse for not doing it in the case of a person who is alleged to be in either a persistent or a minimally conscious state.

The problem I think is twofold, especially in dealing with severe brain injuries: We really do not know what happens in the brains of people who are in these conditions. The technology exists now to start to learn how they deal with things. In fact, it was extraordinarily frustrating for me as one of the attorneys when we were in court and the judges would say how do you intend to prove X? And we would say, "Your Honor, we have these witnesses right here, we can just swear them." "Well, we do not really want to hear about that right now. Let us go on to the next one." And we would say, "Well, we have got these witnesses that we can swear and they can tell you about that." "Well, no, we do not really want to hear about that now." And at the end, what they basically decided is that they did not really care about the evidence because, in the end, people like Terri probably really would not want to live that way anyway.

And so, as Mr. Sedlmeyer pointed out, doctors assume a lot. The medical textbooks are replete with all kinds of quackery that today we recognize as quackery, that 15 years down the road we recognized that we had an obligation to people.

The courts simply do not get it either. They will rely on doctors who, as Dr. Cranford in the Terri Schiavo case pointed out to me, he said, you know, they really did not cross-examine me very well. He said, of course, if somebody would have asked me, I would have said that Terri Schiavo should have been put in a functional MRI machine and we should have seen how her brain worked. But the court would have not gone along with it and neither would Michael Schiavo. Well, the fact of the matter is, as Ms. Adamson put it, we would not starve Scott Petersen to death because under the Geneva Convention that is considered a horrific crime. But in the case of Terri Schiavo, the judge himself recognized that she might have been cognizant of what was happening to her, and we certainly believe that she was.

So what you have here is a debate that focuses on whether people should be allowed to die. Dr. Young talked a lot about the statistics and how many people, and, gee, we really do not want to be getting involved in these processes. Well, the government is involved in these processes. It has been involved for a long time under Medicare and Medicaid. And as a matter of fact, Terri Schiavo, who was not dead yet and who was not dying, was in a hospice. My own view is that somebody ought to be looking at the Medicare and Medicaid problems associated with that one, because beside her brain injury, she was as healthy as a horse and that is why it took her so long to die.

So that what I think we have here in the case of people with disabilities is there is a lot of projection that goes on. People who we might call in other context do-gooders are really paternalistic. And as Ms. Adamson pointed out, all you really need here is for people with disabilities to get the same rights as everyone else. But, you know, we have a system in which people with disabilities and foster kids get lost. And if you look at Terri Schiavo's case, and I know I am out of time and I will be done in 1 second, the Florida Department of Children and Families had an obligation for 15 years to look in on Terri Schiavo, but they lost her just like they lost those kids in foster care. And they could not even show up on the last day at the hearing. They said they were going to be in the Federal court to support us, but they did not even show up for the hearing then. So we have a lot of people paid for with Federal money who are asleep at the switch. I will leave it at that. Thank you, Mr. Chairman.

Mr. SOUDER. Well one of the important things about this panel is that none of us move probably an hour, 30 minutes, without somebody bringing up cost pressures. In other words, when we go back to our offices we will read memos, we will read articles, we will have groups come in on health care. We hear this constantly. And to have a human face on the tradeoffs we make is really important because it is so easy to just move the numbers around and look at the numbers. These are tough decisions because when dollars are spent on high-risk cases, it means there are less dollars for other things, and how we prioritize this. We need to know the human faces and what moral and ethical decisions we are making, and what less than medical knowledge decisions we are making, and how the legal process, Congressman Cummings said earlier, for all kinds of children's cases we have advocates and guardians, how do we work through this kind of process. It is amazingly difficult. But you have really put a human face on this.

Now in a question that we have had several times, and I just want to make sure we get this on the record to clarify, we have had several references today to Scott Petersen, whether or not there is pain, one member said earlier and I heard all over the media, that this is not painful, Ms. Adamson had a little bit different type of testimony, and if you want to start with this one, but even at the end process, if it is so painless, why would we not use that process as opposed to the electric chair? Maybe Mr. Destro can respond. And even if it is painless, if you can drug somebody enough, does that mean it is right? Those are some fundamental questions here. Anybody want to talk to that?

Ms. ADAMSON. Well, that is exactly one of mine. With Terri Schiavo, if she was, in fact, like they are saying, not able to feel anything, then why give her all that morphine?

Ms. Coleman. There is an issue here about end of life, actual end of life care for people who are eminently dying. When my father died of bone cancer, in the last 5 days of his life he stopped consuming; he did not want to drink or eat. And he was in hospice at home and getting very good care. We moistened his mouth and provided the medications. I think that it would have been painful to him to get fluids because he was physiologically shutting down, he was in renal failure.

That is not the same thing as taking away food and water from a healthy person or even an ill person who has still got time ahead of them. What has happened is that some of these bioethicists have conflated these issues. They have gone on television and told everybody that the one situation is the same as the other. And because so many people have been through the other, they think that we are lying. It does not make any sense, but it does seem to be how hard this agenda has been pushed with falsehood, really.

Mr. SOUDER. Mr. Destro.

Mr. DESTRO. Mr. Chairman, if I can just add. I think one of the most telling parts of the Terri Schiavo story is that her guardian, during the period of time in which Terri's law was applicable, he was all over the news media, on CNN, particularly, they had him on, and they really gave the impression that he was a doctor. He did have a doctorate, but his doctorate was in public health and his specialty was in health care finance. He was appointed as Terri Schiavo's guardian. Now why someone with a doctorate and a specialty in health care finance is looking at the brain capabilities of someone in allegedly minimally conscious state, I do not know. But I think that fact alone tells you a big story.

Mr. SOUDER. Mr. Destro, and whoever else on this panel may know the answer to this question, how common are these cases or similar cases, and what numbers are we dealing with? You heard Dr. Young say 2,500 in the one study was an estimate. What familiarity do you have, and what kind of range and type of cases are we talking?

Mr. DESTRO. Well, I think there is a large range of cases. I think if you are talking about people who are in a persistent vegetative state, if you take, on the one extreme, people who are in a coma, and then you take people who are just affected, like my great aunt is, with dementia, the beginning stages of Alzheimer's or dementia, if people are developing these mental disabilities, all you need to do is go down and find the nearest nursing home and walk down the hallways and see how people are treated there. We treat them as warehouse patients. And there is a lot of those cases, and the Federal Government is picking up a lot of the tab. The Schindler family certainly would have been happy if they had sent Terri home. It would have been a lot cheaper to have her at home than if we had had her in this hospice, that I am absolutely sure that the Federal Government paid for.

My point is that I think this population is quite a bit larger than people make it out to be. And it is in the lack of rehab where I have my concerns. We know enough now, U.S. News and World Report, USA Today, all these things are coming out with all the magical ways in which the brain works. And we really do not know what that rehab is doing and what effect that attempt at least to mainstream Mr. Sedlmeyer's daughter is having on her. We will never know unless we can open her up to the point where she can tell us.

Mr. SOUDER. Ms. Watson.

Ms. WATSON. I guess it is attorney Destro?

Mr. DESTRO. Yes, ma'am.

Ms. WATSON. What are you asking of Congress? As an attorney, are you asking us something along legal lines to determine when a person gets cutoff from life support? Are you asking for us to play role in the decisions? It is not clear to me. I would like to take this off of the Terri Schiavo case; that is one case. And as I understand, there are thousands of them. I am trying, for my own edification, to see what role people out there want Congress to play in these decisions. So as an attorney, can you enlighten us. What is it that you would be seeking?

Mr. DESTRO. That is a very good question. I appreciate your asking it. I think if we had a clearer answer in the Schiavo statute, it would have been helpful. What I would say is that we want to make sure that for every Federal dollar spent the patient or the patient's advocate—and in cases where there are not advocates for the patient, that there should be some—that the patient or the patient's advocate has the highest level of informed consent and procedural due process possible. If we go back many, many, many moons to one of the worst civil rights cases that has ever been decided, which is Dred Scott, Justice Tawney talked about Black people not having any rights that White people were bound to respect. And what I am telling you is that it is in the process, that is why we have a due process clause, it is in the process by which we deal with people with disabilities that I think the discrimination takes place. And so what I would like to see Congress do is craft some rules that talk about the process that you go through in the decisionmaking process.

Ms. WATSON. Relative to State courts, district courts? I am trying to pin down—see, this was an individual case.

Mr. DESTRO. Yes.

Ms. WATSON. And I am not sure if we had a role to play in that decision. There has been a lot of critique on the various levels of courts that were involved in this decision. And so, as an attorney, when you say an "advocate," this would not be the guardian, this would not be the family, this would not be the medical professional. I am trying in my mind to narrow down what role, what responsibility we have. And are you talking about changing the courts? What is it that you see there is a gap or a loop and we need to fill it?

Mr. DESTRO. Well the first gap would be in hotly disputed cases, like you had. I would suggest strongly that you amend the habeas corpus rules to allow for a due process review, just like you would in a Scott Petersen case. But on the other end of the spectrum, I think that we desperately need in Federal programs training for judges, for advocates, for court-appointed special advocates, and for guardian ad litem with respect to the reality of the problems of people with disabilities. And that I do think is an appropriate Federal role.

Mr. SOUDER. Ms. Watson, could you let Ms. Coleman respond.

Ms. WATSON. Yes, Ms. Coleman.

Ms. Coleman. To answer part of the question with a study, there have been a number of studies of caregiver family members of people with Alzheimer's, in one that was reported last year, it was about the sixth of such, it had found that the caregiver family member underrated the quality of life of the individual with Alzheimer's lower than the person themself rated their own quality of life with Alzheimer's. This sixth study tried to figure out why. And they learned that the caregiver was projecting their own personal misery at the burdens of caregiving onto their relative and thereby underrating their quality of life.

Now the disability community has been kind of locked out of all these discussions. But I just want to say, to coin a popular phrase, well Duh. We know this. This is the way the world is, that it is not uncommon. Many caregivers are not like my co-presenter here today. So people with disabilities feel that we need protection, legal protection for those situations where our existence is not respected, be it by family members, health care providers, all kinds of folks. We still feel that our rights deserve, we deserve equality under the law, and there should not be a cognitive test for personhood under the Constitution of the United States.

Ms. WATSON. Many years ago, Public Law 94–142 specified, and I think you might know that, in education what needed to be done for the disabled. And I feel the disability community has been very strong and up to the challenge in the past. What I am trying to get out, and maybe this panel is not the right one, and maybe this committee is not the committee, maybe it should go to Judiciary, what is it that all of you here who came to testify would like to see us do at the Federal level in terms of refining the law? We do not make laws for the States; we do over-arching laws that are national. So, what is it that you would like to see us do for the disabled community? Can anyone address that?

Ms. Coleman. I think that what we have been trying to do is come together as a community, the same groups and others as the ones you were referencing who worked on Public Law 94–142, but we have not yet had the time, given the rush of this process, to really try to bring together all the diverse communities both within and without the disability community to iron out what do we think would work best.

We do think that there needs to be some kind of substantive standard. We would certainly be willing to look at what Congressman Weldon was talking about earlier today, and perhaps there are other ideas, and we would like to be able to bring them back in an appropriate way, perhaps the committee that you are suggesting, Judiciary. We are here to work this through.

I do not think there are really easy answers about the substantive response. I do think, though, that we need information and data that has not been collected. We feel that the failure to collect that data has been, to some extent, engineered by the bioethics agenda, which is about creating a standard for health care rationing we think that has to do with based on disability. We would like to see that looked at and sorted through and get real data to work with.

Ms. WATSON. Maybe let me just suggest, if I have a minute, Mr. Chairman, Danny Davis, Representative from Illinois, has H.R. 910, but it deals with Medicaid and community-based attendant services.

Ms. Coleman. MiCASSA. We support that.

Ms. WATSON. Yes. And I would think you might want to get in touch with the sponsor of this bill. It is moving I guess on a track, but you would have time, I am sure, to meet with your communities and maybe suggest some amendments if this is not inclusive enough. You might want to get in touch with office as to some ideas that the Association comes up with.

Ms. Coleman. I think we will talk to the group that is the lead sponsor of that. I am from Illinois, so it was actually Congressman Davis that helped me connect up with this hearing today.

Ms. WATSON. Thank you, Mr. Chairman.

Mr. SOUDER. Thank you. Mr. Cummings? And I know, Ms. Coleman, if you need to leave, you have a plane.

Ms. Coleman. Yes, I do. Thank you.

Mr. CUMMINGS. Mr. Coleman, if you leave, I just wanted to thank you. And I want to say to all of you, I thank you for your testimony. I think the sad part about this entire thing is all about we are in a political atmosphere. I think politics has just made this total thing a mess. And the sad part about it is that a lot of times when you get the political piece in it, you forget about the disabilities community that you talked about. I know that when this issue came before us, a lot of us did not like the idea that it was brought before us, but we had to make decisions. It was a tough decision, talking about Schiavo now, and the interesting thing is that I think most Members of Congress when they look at this from a disabilities standpoint, they have to at least pause and say let us really look at this very carefully. The sad part about it is that when the politics comes in, the considerations become more difficult to make because it all becomes a part of a whole ball of wax, sadly.

What I am saying to you is, I listened very carefully to Ms. Watson's questions, and one of the things I thought about as she was asking the question, I think we all want to, I am sure Chairman Souder does too, want to come to some conclusions and try to figure out how do we be fair and protect those who are vulnerable. All of you, the stories have been just incredible.

Ms. ADAMSON. Mr. Cummings, could I say something?

Mr. CUMMINGS. Sure.

Ms. ADAMSON. I want to mention, I have had an incredible recovery. I am still paralyzed, but I have had 10 years in and out of rehab. Had it not been for my husband being an attorney and screaming and yelling to get the insurance company and the doctors to give me treatment—and I had private insurance, now look at the people who do not have any insurance—they wanted to ship me off to a skilled nursing facility. I cannot tell you around the world how many e-mails I get from families who are told this is a hopeless situation, give up, and the families do not want to give up. And had it not been for my husband fighting for me, and then I had to be willing to do the rehab not knowing if I would ever get better. I think that was the most scariest thing for me, not having the answers but trusting that I just had to live in the moment and take it day by day and give it my best effort. So you are looking at somebody who has had a lot of rehab. Unfortunately, people that do not have health care insurance, they do not have an advocate who is that squeaky wheel, do get shipped off and warehoused.

Mr. CUMMINGS. And not only get shipped off and warehoused, but often die.

Ms. ADAMSON. Yes. And what is scary, too, is that rehabilitation program that I went into in 1995 is no longer available; 20, 30 years ago, a patient would be looking at 9 months in the hospital to recover.

Mr. CUMMINGS. Excuse me. Dr. Coleman, I understand. You look like you are trying to be very polite, but we do not want you to be so polite that you miss your plane.

Ms. COLEMAN. Thank you.

Mr. CUMMINGS. Excuse me, Ms. Adamson.

Ms. ADAMSON. But I wanted to say—what was I saying?

Mr. CUMMINGS. You were just talking about your rehabilitation and a program that no longer exists that existed back then.

Ms. ADAMSON. Right. Now, you are lucky if you can get 6 weeks and they want you out. That is the scariest thing to me. Based on the fact that I was 33, they looked at it, as opposed to someone who was in their 70's or 80's, I got turned down by rehabilitation as well because they felt that I had no chance of recovery. And I went in on the spinal cord team, not the stroke team, because of my condition. So had I not had an advocate who was going to fight, I would not be sitting here.

Mr. CUMMINGS. I think that Senator Obama has an expression that I would use so often, and it is just so accurate. He says, "Sometimes in our society we have an empathy deficit." I think that we need to figure out how it is that we can be fair to all of us, period, to ourselves. It seems like everybody kind of thinks that they will never find themselves in these positions, or they will never have a family member in these positions, and so they kind of just float on down the road. But these things are happening every day.

I really do appreciate you all coming in and telling the Nation and telling us about your situations. I think it has to cause all of us to just pause and figure out, again, like I said, what we can do to be fair, to make sure that we are not just guided by financial considerations. Because let me tell you something, if it is just finance, a whole lot of people are going down the drain, period. I think we have to also look at how is it that we can look at our Medicare/Medicaid system and see what it is that we can do within that system to try to come up with that fairness and value everybody's life.

Mr. Sedlmeyer, I want to thank you, too. When I listened to your testimony, I could not help but be moved when you said one of your favorite roles is being a father. I can relate. I think you said a lot for fatherhood and your wife has said a lot for motherhood, too. I am just glad that you were here to share your story, and you too.

Mr. DESTRO. Mr. Cummings, if I could just add something just briefly. I think that in one respect the question really is not how can we be fair. I think the question is really how can we be informed and how can caregivers be informed. As a matter of informed consent, all of us have the right to choose. But the choice should be based on facts out there. And I think that the Federal Government has a superb role to play in making sure that caregivers are well-informed. If there is going to be Medicare or Medicaid payment, that the caregivers need to be trained and they need to be well-informed.

I found out during the course of the Schiavo litigation that just a superb judge in King County, WA, set up the court-appointed Special Advocate Program because he noticed that in juvenile courts these people in guardianship proceedings just were not getting good representation, either by the attorneys or by their special advocates. And so what he set up was a training program. And it seems to me that judges have to do mandatory continuing judicial education, lawyers have to do mandatory continuing education. It seems to me that we would all be better off if we understood the nature of these conditions. And I think that is something that you all could really do. Thank you.

Mr. CUMMINGS. I know in our State courts we have quite a few judges in each county. In Baltimore, for example, there may be 35 judges and 2 or 3 of them are assigned to these kinds of cases. So it would not necessarily require the training of all the judges, but some who would deal with these.

Mr. Chairman, as I close, I would just ask unanimous consent that the statement of Arthur Kaplan with the Department of Medical Ethics, University of Pennsylvania, be admitted. We had wanted him to appear but he could not. And that the case of *Cruzan* v. *Director, Missouri Department of Health,* a Supreme Court case, 497 U.S. 261, be made a part of the record.

Mr. SOUDER. Without objection, so ordered.

Congresswoman Watson, do you have anything?

Ms. WATSON. Yes. I, too, would like to thank all of those who took the time to come today. I represent the State of California, Los Angeles, and I served as chair of the health and human services committee for 17 years. We had cases like this in front of us often. So what we did, what I did was carry legislation to require every single hospital to have a biomedical committee that would discuss these end of life issues. As was said by Representative Cummings, we are political figures and very few sitting in our chambers, I was in the Senate, were medical doctors. But we required every hospital that served the public to have a biomedical committee to discuss these ethical and moral issues. It was very difficult to deal with them from our position.

No. 2, we argued against allowing the HMO movement, health maintenance organizations, because, Ms. Adamson, they did control the amount of hours and time, you would dial into a number and the person at the other end can tell you whether that is a particular service or procedure that could be provided. And I think there was something wrong with that. What we did, we had to put it into the hands of those people who were trained. So I carried legislation that said we should have informed consent when you do an invasive treatment, so that the patient along with the provider could exchange information and raise the right questions, so when a patient made a decision to go ahead, that patient would know all about it. So there are a lot of things that need to be done. The problem is we have 50 States.

Ms. ADAMSON. I am in California, too.

Ms. WATSON. So I am trying to glean out of this, Mr. Chairman, just what we can do. Also in our State, we have continuous education required for not only our justices, but our judges and attorneys at will. But it is always out there. You know, there are new technologies, new medical provisions, and methods and so on that change rapidly. And so how you grapple with this and not get specific to an individual case is really a challenge that we have.

So, if any of you, or all of you, would like to write to me and enlighten me on what we could do, I would be happy to consider it. Because, believe me, and I am sure the Chair also, there are so many, on this Schiavo case, there are so many intricate facts that we just do not know, and I understand it was heard before 24 judges in 6 courts, and there was representation on both sides, and so on. So I wanted to get away from a specific case, not having all the facts and not having all the professionals in front of us. But I would entertain any kind of information you provide me with.

Ms. ADAMSON. Well we may just have to do lunch because I am from Los Angeles. I may write to you. [Laughter.]

Ms. WATSON. Good, and I would welcome that to help us through this.

Ms. ADAMSON. I think, yes, we need to clarify the rights of the disabled.

Ms. WATSON. Thank you, Mr. Chairman.

Mr. SOUDER. Do any of the witnesses have any closing comments?

Mr. DESTRO. I do have one, and that is, I think we should make sure that we try and understand that not all of the things we are talking about are very expensive. One of the things I have learned in watching my wife, who has a doctorate in social work, work through a national training program on adoption awareness, crisis pregnancy counselling for women with unplanned pregnancies, is that many times the advocates simply just do not know. And these training programs are extraordinarily cost-effective. And in the course of that, I came to know an excellent nurse practitioner who has done quite an interesting job in training judges, domestic relations judges. One of the most effective ways of judges keeping control of violent people in their courtroom, which we saw down in Georgia, is to have some food, crackers, in their drawer, because people who have a can of coke or some crackers to munch on do not shoot people.

Ms. WATSON. Give them some chocolate.

Mr. DESTRO. Exactly. And it makes them feel good. But a lot of this stuff is a lot more cost-effective if you give control back to people and do not leave it in the hands of the so-called experts and committees. As my former colleague and friend on the Civil Rights Commission, Mary Frances Barry said during a discussion of AIDS related discrimination about 15 years ago, and she pointed right at one of the bioethicists, and I will leave his name out of the record today, and she said, "How do you get to be one of those? Do you just hang your shingle out and become a bioethicist?" There is no question that there is an ideology there and that it is at odds with what I believe are the duties that we all have to our neighbors and friends with disabilities. They are more concerned about the finances than we are. So it seems to me that a lot of the stuff that we can do is actually pretty cheap and cost-effective if you just give it back to people and let them use their ingenuity. Thank you.

Mr. SOUDER. Mr. Sedlmeyer, do you have any comments?

Mr. SEDLMEYER. Am I on? Yes, I would like to make a comment. I would like to direct it to Ms. Watson, because you have said more than once tell us how we can help you, tell us what we can do. And from my perspective as a caregiver, I would like to suggest two things that you might be able to do.

One, of course, and I know we are very limited on this, but money does make a big difference. Having the funds available to give the care that is needed to one that you love is indispensable. And it is through programs like the Medicaid Waiver Program that we have been able to keep Valerie at home. And I know you have to make difficult decisions on budgeting, and I know the Medicaid funds to the States have been reduced, and we understand and we are willing to make those kinds of financial sacrifices to keep our daughter at home. But as you pondering your budgets, your Medicaid, your Medicare budget, please keep in mind those programs that may in the long run yield beneficial results in terms of the bottom line. I think the longer we can keep Valerie at home with us, the better it will be for everyone—her, us, and the whole health care system.

Second, I have heard Mr. Cummings address this, you all say you are political creatures. But you know what? You are leaders of this Nation and your perspective on issues of this magnitude is important. In a sense, you all have bully pulpits. And one of the things that really concerned me early in Valerie's life, it was at the point where her feeding tube was going to be inserted—I did not say this in my testimony, but Valerie is a twin, her twin sister is Vanessa, Vanessa is perfect in every way—my pediatrician came up to me before the surgery and he said to me, "If something goes wrong during the surgery, what do you want me to do?" And I looked at him and I said, "I want you to do the same thing that you would do for her sister." So, you see, in some sense it is all a matter of perception.

I believe you in Congress and you in the Senate have the ability because of your positions, because of your access to the media, because you have a strong voice in this Nation, you can change the perception of people in our Nation to treat, as we have heard all the other ones on this panel say, we do not want special rights either as individuals or for our children, we just want the same civil rights as everyone else.

Mr. SOUDER. Thank you very much. And I think on that note we will conclude. I want to thank Ms. Adamson, too. I watched you multiple times on television during the national debates, as well as Mr. Destro.

We are in an interesting situation here in Congress. Had we been discussing this issue a few weeks ago, everybody in the world would have been focused very closely. But this is the real business of how we govern, not kind of a TV show. We had both good and bad come out of that whole process in Florida. The good thing was we had some public discussion and kind of first awareness. The bad thing is now people are so confused that it may be more difficult in fact to move legislation.

It got into the political arena, which happens with any bill we move through. But we knew potentially by coming back that Sunday night, when were in a very kind of end of the alternative road, that it was going to get to become a political football, which it did. All of a sudden what was bipartisan support and trying to deal with the broader issue became focused on one case, very confused, and family questions, what did the judges see and not see. And in reality, we have to learn from that experience, when it was an experience that was so public that now people are just loaded with opinions that may or may not be factual, and all of us are confused, Members of Congress are confused, because we all tended to choose sides and only wanted to get the information that came from that side.

Now we have to try to sort through actual legislation and go back and kind of reinvent the wheel to where we were before the case, but with now a much more quasi-informed public, quasi-informed Members, and at the same time everybody understanding we have some problems around the country. Often, these types of cases, sometimes it was like, as I argue, the Judge Thomas hearings for the Supreme Court did more to define sexual harassment in America, which was not necessarily relevant to anything he did, but because people watched the debate, people changed their behaviors and they started to adjust and learn.

Hopefully, as an oversight committee, this helps move that forward. As legislation moves, it will move through different committees, and in our HHS oversight we will continue to look at this, and we also have Justice Department oversight. So as we look at this among the many issues we deal with, this has been a very helpful first hearing for you to put a human face on it, and we thank you very much for taking thc time to do so.

With that, this subcommittee stands adjourned.

[Whereupon, at 4:52 p.m., the subcommittee was adjourned.]

[Additional information submitted for the hearing record follows:]

PROTECTING AMERICA'S ELDERS: A CALL TO ACTION

By Ken Connor
Chairman, Center for a Just Society

This afternoon, I'd like to talk with you about the problems of the elderly in America. It's a matter I've been greatly concerned about, not simply because of my own advancing age, but because, for more than 20 years, as a trial lawyer I've been involved in representing victims of abuse and neglect in nursing homes around the country and have seen some of the saddest cases imaginable. In addition, I served on Florida's Task Force for the Availability and Affordability of Long Term Care, where we engaged in a very intensive study of the problems of the elderly and recommended some solutions aimed at mitigating some of those problems.

As a father of four and as a trial lawyer, I can tell you that my experience is that some of the most profound truths that resonate with the human spirit are to be found in bedtime stories. I made it a practice when my children were young to read them everything from Aesop's Fables to Uncle Remus. In the process of doing that, I realized that these stories often were valuable vehicles for helping juries to understand complicated issues in cases. I'd like to share with you this afternoon at least part of a story that's one of my favorite bedtime stories-one that I hope you will keep in the back of your mind as you reflect upon the way we view, and the way we treat, the elderly in America.

If you have children, then you may already be familiar with the Velveteen Rabbit by Margery Williams. It's really quite a wonderful story:

There was once a velveteen rabbit, and in the beginning he was really splendid. He was fat and bunchy, as a rabbit should be; his coat was spotted brown and white, he had real thread whiskers, and his ears were lined with pink sateen.1

Now, the storyteller goes on to explain how this rabbit was a gift to a young boy, a Christmas gift that was found at the top of a stocking. But as is often the case where children get so many gifts, the rabbit wound up relegated to the children's nursery. In the children's nursery, he came into contact with many, many other toys. The mechanical toys, in particular, had a very superior attitude and they treated this little creature, who was really quite simply made, with some disdain. This was rather depressing to the Velveteen Rabbit, and the only one who was kind to him was the old Skin Horse, a veteran of the nursery. At night, all of these wind-up toys would proudly march around and strut, and the mechanical boat would blow its whistle, and the jointed, wooden lion would pretend to be Real, and all of these toys would pretend to be Real.

And this dialogue took place between the Velveteen Rabbit and the Skin Horse:
"What is REAL?" asked the Rabbit one day, when they were lying side by side near the nursery fender, before Nana came to tidy the room.
"Does it mean having things that buzz inside you and a stick-out handle?"
"Real isn't how you're made," said the Skin Horse. "It's a thing that happens to you. When

a child loves you for a long, long time, not just to play with, but REALLY loves you, then you become Real."
"Does it hurt?" asked the Rabbit.
"Sometimes," said the Skin Horse, for he was always truthful. "When you are Real you don't mind being hurt."
"Does it happen all at once, like being wound up," he asked, "or bit by bit?"
"It doesn't happen all at once," said the Skin Horse. "You become. It takes a long time. That's why it doesn't happen often to people who break easily, or have sharp edges, or who have to be carefully kept. Generally, by the time you are Real, most of your hair has been loved off, and your eyes drop out and you get loose in your joints and very shabby. But these things don't matter at all, because once you are Real you can't be ugly, except to people who don't understand."2

Then over the course of time, the storyteller goes on to talk about how this rabbit became the favorite of the little boy in the nursery. The boy hugged him tightly and dragged him all over the nursery, and all over the yard, and the rabbit became quite dingy and dirty and, over the course of time, quite shabby. The storyteller goes on to tell us:
Weeks passed, and the little Rabbit grew very old ... and his brown spots faded. He even began to lose his shape, and he scarcely looked like a rabbit any more, except to the Boy. To him he was always beautiful, and that was all that the little Rabbit cared about. He didn't mind how he looked to other people, because the nursery magic had made him Real, and when you are Real shabbiness doesn't matter3.

THE THREAT OF THE 'DISPOSABLE MAN ETHIC

Now, folks, in the story, we see that when the rabbit begins to deteriorate with the passage of time, he becomes special and valued all the more. But that's in the story. In the real world in which we live today, often the very opposite takes place. Indeed, I would suggest to you that there is no class of people, other than the unborn, who are more threatened by our current "disposable man" ethic that we as a culture have developed in the aftermath of Roe v. Wade-the ethic that diminishes the value of human life-than the elderly.

Wesley J. Smith, in his profound book, Culture of Death: The Assault on Medical Ethics in America, made this statement: Our culture is fast devolving into one in which killing is beneficent, suicide is rational, natural death is undignified, and caring properly and compassionately for people who are elderly ... disabled, despairing or dying, is a burden that wastes emotional and financial resources.4

Indeed, if you listen to Joseph Fletcher, the now-dead situational ethicist, he suggested a list of 15 indicators that he hoped would be used by society to divide it between individuals who possessed true "humanhood" and those who did not. He wanted to distinguish between "truly human beings," deserving of great moral concern, and others who were "subpersonal" and of little concern.5 Think of these criteria as they relate to the Velveteen Rabbit and to the elderly in our society. Among the criteria he said it takes to qualify for being "truly human" are: minimum intelligence, self-awareness, self-control, a sense of futurity, memory, concern for others, communication, and neocortical function.6

How many Alzheimer's patients, do you think, could meet those criteria? How many people with advanced dementia? How many people who populate our nursing homes and long-term care facilities would qualify for "personhood" status using these indicators? How many of these people would be treasured as being "Real" in this real world in which we live?

THE IMPENDING CRISIS-A LOOK AT THE NUMBERS

Let me give you some statistics that I think will help you put this in perspective. Currently, we have 35 million people in this country who are 65 or older.7 In the next 30 years, that number is expected to double to 70 million.8 The 65-74 age group will rise 89 percent; the 75-84 age group will rise 119 percent.9 The over 85 age group, which is the fastest growing age group in the country, will rise 143 percent.10 Two-thirds of the people in that age group (over 85) are going to need long-term care.11 Currently, we have 1.5 million residents populating 17,000 nursing homes in this country.12 That number will likely double to 3 million by 2035.

Let's evaluate the costs. When Lyndon Johnson passed his agenda for the Great Society, Medicare and Medicaid were part of the package. Medicare's cost in 1967, shortly after its enactment, was approximately $1 billion.13 But in the year 2000, the cost was approximately $300 billion.14 Medicaid spending in 1967 was approximately $1 billion, but in 2000 it was approximately $200 billion.15 Now keep in mind that only 9 percent of Medicaid patients use long-term care benefits, but they account for 43 percent of Medicaid costs!16 This is because Medicaid provides coverage for two-thirds of all nursing home patients and about half of all nursing home costs.17 Americans over 65 today cost Medicaid $8,704 per year.18 They represent only 25 percent of the Medicaid population, but they account for 75 percent of the cost.19 By the year 2030 in today's costs, each woman will need $124,370 worth of long-term care.20 Men, not because they are any less valuable but because they die younger, will only require $56,895 in today's costs.21 Medicaid already accounts for about 20 to 25 percent of all state spending.22 Now, I want you to reflect on this in terms of the dynamic that is going to be taking place. When the baby boomers retire, of which I'm one, the estimated Medicaid costs in real dollars are likely to quadruple. That means that by 2020 or 2030, Medicaid could consume the entire budget of every state in the union.23 Can you imagine the implications of that?

Let's look at the Social Security implications. In 1950, we had 16 workers for every retiree. 24 Today, we have three workers for every retiree, and that ratio is quickly changing to 2 to 1.25 I would submit to you that this data has profound implications for the elderly in a culture which increasingly calculates an individual's net worth in terms of cost/benefit analyses, quality of life assessments, and functional capacity studies. How long do you think it will be before the youth of America, bending under the weight of ever-increasing costs for Medicare, Medicaid, and the burdens of Social Security-those youth who have been raised on the "disposable man" ethic that flows out of Roe v. Wade-how long do you think it will be before that group concludes as John Whitehead has suggested, that the elderly are just "useless eaters" and quite unwanted? We hear much today about class warfare and age discrimination. You ain't seen nothing yet! Wait 'til these pressures come to full flower within the next 30 years.

THE PLIGHT OF THE ELDERLY: DISTURBING TRENDS

Today, I'd like to expand your thinking a little bit, if I may, about the problems of the elderly. Now, when pro-life and pro-family groups think about sanctity of life issues and the elderly, their thinking typically begins and ends with euthanasia. Now, we had a big setback today in the federal district court in Oregon, where a federal judge struck down the attorney general's order that physicians who intentionally prescribe deadly doses of federally controlled substances in order to facilitate suicide are in violation of the Controlled Substances Act. So, it's understandable that we would register our concerns about euthanasia. Indeed, euthanasia is a very real and present danger in this country, and all you have to do is look at the experience in the Netherlands to see just how dangerous it really is.

But sadly, what is virtually overlooked completely by pro-life, pro-family groups, by many policy makers and public advocates, what is ignored by so many of these is the plight of the 1.5 million people who now reside in nursing homes in this country. These forgotten, frail elderly often suffer from terminal loneliness and are all too often victims of abuse and neglect. Let me offer you some illustrations, which I will acknowledge are anecdotal, but which I think are important for you to consider in terms of evaluating some very disturbing trends that we're experiencing in this country. I promise you that I'll connect it up with data and that we won't simply stick with war stories.

MORRIS CAMPBELL

The very first case that I tried, probably the first nursing home abuse and neglect case tried in Florida, involved a fellow by the name of Morris Campbell, a 60-plus-year-old stroke victim, who was admitted to a nursing home owned by the famous Chicago Bears running back, Walter Payton. Walter was affectionately known as "Sweetness" among his teammates, but he didn't enjoy that reputation down in Lakeland, where his nursing home was. Indeed, around the time of Mr. Campbell's admission, the home had several moratoriums against new admissions imposed because of substandard conditions. Over the course of time, Mr. Campbell, who was a stroke victim and who was incontinent of bowel and bladder, wound up contracting pressure sores. Eventually, he developed multiple, massive, infected, necrotic bedsores, which produced a generalized blood stream infection that caused his death. When I tried Mr. Campbell's case, I thought that surely this had to be an isolated incident.

CHARLES FRYE

But it wasn't long before someone who read about the Campbell case in a newspaper contacted me about the problems of their father, Charles Frye, who was in a nursing home in the Spring Hill, Fla., area. Mr. Frye was an elderly man, who, like Mr. Campbell, was the victim of a stroke. Because his caregivers hadn't provided him with range of motion exercises, he became contracted in all of his limbs. And because the nursing home was short-staffed, and didn't have time to turn and reposition patients, he, too, developed pressure sores. As a consequence of that, he had both legs amputated, simply because of pressure sores. Later on, because his arms contracted and his hands came to rest under his chin, and because the nursing home responsible for caring for him failed to put a pressure-relieving device much like a Nerf ball between his chin and his hand, his right hand had to be amputated. And because he was incontinent of bladder, he had to be catheterized. And because he received poor quality catheter care, his genitals had to be amputated. The nursing home staff came to Mrs. Frye and said, "Can't you see? Your husband is trying to die. We should let him go."

Now folks, I can tell you that no one suffers more from what President Bush has called the "soft bigotry of low expectations" than the elderly. People assume that old age and ill health necessarily mean skin breakdowns. It ain't necessarily so. Mrs. Frye took her husband home, assumed responsibility for his care, and over the next three years, Mr. Frye never suffered a single skin breakdown. In the process of caring for him, however, she ruined her own health.

Mr. Campbell's and Mr. Frye's cases were the first two cases I was involved with, and over the years, I handled numerous other cases that had many common elements-bedsores, malnutrition, dehydration, and residents languishing in urine and feces.

JOHN LEE BUTLER

Among the last two cases I handled was a case involving an elderly black gentleman by the name of John Lee Butler, who, after having been mugged by some desperados, suffered a brain injury. He ultimately wound up in a nursing home in Tampa. The conditions in the home were deplorable. In addition to widespread insect infestations, maggots were found in mattresses and the stench of urine was so overpowering that visitors could smell it from the parking lot. Mr. Butler suffered more than 30 falls in the nursing home. He also developed 11 pressure sores, became dehydrated, and died. His death certificate said he died from "emaciation." The testimony in that case was that he was a slow eater who had difficulty swallowing, and the staff didn't take time to feed him. They often picked up his tray completely untouched and took it back to the kitchen. Sometimes, they ate the food themselves.

LETHA COLLINS

And then finally, Letha Collins was a stroke victim admitted to a nursing home in Perry, Fla. She was sexually assaulted-twice-by a predator who was also a resident of the nursing home. The nursing home suppressed that information the first time, never notifying the family or the police. Mrs. Collins was beaten with a shoe once by another resident who had a history of violent behavior in the nursing home. Ultimately, Mrs. Collins suffered from malnutrition and died from dehydration after having lived with a terrible vaginal infection for months-one that was completely avoidable and curable. The stench of that infection was so great that the testimony in the case was that you could smell her before you could see her.

ELDER ABUSE AND NEGLECT: A NATIONAL PROBLEM

These stories may be anecdotal, but they are symptomatic of a larger problem facing the institutionalized elderly. Sadly, neglect and abuse are all too often part of the daily

existence of many, not all, but many of the institutionalized elderly.
In fact, in a recent report prepared by the Minority Staff of the Special Investigations Division of the Committee on Government Reform for the U.S. House of Representatives, it was revealed that almost one out of every three U.S. nursing homes were cited for an abuse violation in the two-year period between January 1, 1999, and January 1, 2001.26 All of the violations that were cited in the report, which was released after a series of investigations27 of the incidence of physical, sexual, and verbal abuse in nursing homes nationwide, had at least the potential to harm nursing home residents. In more than 1,600 of these homes, the abuse violations were serious enough to cause actual harm to residents or to place them in immediate jeopardy of death or serious injury.28
Now hear this: The committee found that in this country, the percentage of nursing homes with abuse violations is increasing. The percentage of nursing homes cited for abuse violations in annual inspections has tripled just since 1996.29 Tripled!!
In March 2002, the U.S. Government Accounting Office released a report that made the following observations:

Allegations of physical and sexual abuse of nursing home residents frequently are not reported promptly. Local law enforcement officials indicated that they are seldom summoned to nursing homes to immediately investigate allegations of physical or sexual abuse. Some of these officials indicated that they often receive such reports after the evidence has been compromised. Although abuse allegations should be reported to state survey agencies immediately, they often are not.30

Now imagine, folks, the howls of indignation that you would be hearing from policymakers, pundits and public advocates if this were happening in the day care centers of America. But sadly, because it happens to the elderly, the public's voice is all too often muted. The GAO report goes on to say: Safeguards to protect residents from potentially abusive individuals are insufficient at both the federal and state level. There is no federal statute requiring criminal background checks of nursing home employees nor does CMS [Centers for Medicare and Medicaid Services] require them. ... Safeguards at the state level are also insufficient. While nursing homes are responsible for protecting residents from abuse, survey agencies in the states we visited rarely recommended that certain sanctions-such as civil monetary penalties or terminations from federal programs-be imposed.31

INDICATORS OF BETTER NURSING HOME CARE

Staffing levels are critical to outcomes by patients in long-term care facilities. In fact, staffing levels are the single biggest predictor of outcomes for residents in terms of their skin integrity, nutrition and hydration. The more staff they have, the better the outcome. Nursing homes with low staffing levels tend to have major problems with nutritional issues and pressure sores. Nevertheless, a recent HCFA (CMS) report revealed that more than 92 percent-more than 9 out of 10 of the nation's nursing homes-have too few workers to take proper care of their residents.32 Can you imagine that? And in a study recently conducted of 600 nursing home employees, almost 40 percent-and this is self-reporting- 40 percent acknowledged that they had committed at least one psychologically abusive act in the past year and 10 percent acknowledged that they had physically abused a patient in the last year.33 Notwithstanding all of this, the U.S. Government Accounting Office has reported that incidents of abuse are under-reported and uninvestigated all too often.

FAITH-BASED AND NONPROFIT FACILITIES

Now let's talk about the value of faith-based initiatives and their relationship to the crisis of care in the nursing home industry. Now, you're talking to a guy who, as an economics major, has historically been an advocate of free markets and I remain such today. This part will be very controversial for those of you who, as I, have been market-based and market-driven. I'm not affirming the facts that I am about to call to your attention-I'm simply going to report the facts as they were reported in the September 2001 American Journal of Public Health. Two-thirds of the nursing homes in this country are investor-owned. The study published in the American Journal examined whether investor ownership affects the quality of care. Here's what the researchers concluded: In analyzing 1998 data from 13,693 nursing homes-remember there are only 17,000 in the country, so we have a pretty big sample here-the results showed that investor-owned facilities averaged 46.5 percent more deficiencies per home than in nonprofit facilities. 34 (Deficiencies refer to violations of the federal code aimed at protecting nursing home residents). The researchers noted:

Our results suggest that investor-owned nursing homes deliver lower quality care than do nonprofit or public facilities. Moreover, investor-owned facilities usually are part of a chain, and chain ownership per se is associated with a further decrement in quality.35

In short, the report concluded that investor-owned nursing homes provided worse care and less nursing care than do not-for-profit or government-owned facilities.

Now, in Florida, I can tell you that the homes with the worst records of care are investor-owned facilities-and this is not anecdotal, this is the data. Researchers found that "Nurse staffing was lower at investor-owned nursing homes for each occupational category. ... Skimping on staffing by for-profit homes may partly explain their lower quality. ... The most obvious explanation for our findings is that profit-seeking diverts funds and focus from clinical care."36 This report went on to conclude, "We believe it is unwise to entrust such vulnerable patients to profit-seeking firms."37 That's a pretty shocking conclusion-it is counter-intuitive for many of us.

In contrast, I can tell you that the nursing homes with the best records of care are the faith-based homes: the Catholic nursing homes, the Jewish Homes for the Aged, and the like. Now let me say this to those who maintain that we should excise references to our religious faith from the public debate: I believe that by doing so, we impoverish the public discourse on matters relating to human dignity. The Jewish and Christian religious traditions extol the virtue and value of the elderly: "What is man, that thou art mindful of him?"38 We are created in God's image.39 In the book of James, we are told that, "Religion that God our Father accepts as pure and faultless is this: to look after orphans and widows in their distress."40 In I Timothy, the writer exhorts the readers to "Give proper recognition to those widows who are really in need. But if a widow has children or grandchildren, these should learn first of all to put their religion into practice by caring for their own family and so repaying their parents and grandparents, for this is pleasing to God."41 Deuteronomy 5:16 says, "Honor your father and your mother."42 And let me share just one more: "Listen to your father, who gave you life, and do not despise your mother when she is old."43

The arguments of Joseph Fletcher, which have been embraced in large part by the bioethics community, and which threaten to undermine human dignity, have no place in the Judeo-Christian worldview. My hope and goal, Lord willing, is that those arguments will be displaced by those of us who affirm essential human dignity and who believe that men and women, boys and girls, embryo and elderly alike, are created in God's image and therefore, are invested with inherent worth and value. The sad reality is that America's experiment in institutionalizing the elderly is a failed one. I submit to you that the way we treat our elderly here in America is a national scandal. It is America's dirty secret-one that too few are willing to talk about. The whole purpose of my presentation to you is to provoke a discussion about the problem.

PUBLIC POLICY INITIATIVES FOR A BRIGHTER FUTURE

Well, what can we do to correct the problem? What can we do to help ameliorate the situation from a public policy standpoint?

ZERO TOLERANCE FOR ABUSE AND NEGLECT

First of all, I think we must advocate zero-tolerance for abuse and neglect of the elderly in our long-term care facilities. Members of Congress and the President of the United States should be leading the way on these issues. We should be prosecuting offenders; we should be punishing the facilities. One very simple thing we can do is to install so-called "granny cams." I didn't bring them for you today, but I have in my office a compendium of documentary videotapes that show nursing home staff abusing residents on videotape. The nursing staff didn't know they were being videotaped. I recommended installation of cameras in residents' rooms in Florida. The Florida Senate passed a bill approving of the installation of cameras in nursing homes, but the measure died in the House. Nonetheless, believe me, folks, when I say that the behavioral changes that flow from people knowing they are under scrutiny are amazing.

FOSTERING HOME- AND COMMUNITY-BASED ALTERNATIVES

We should promote an array of options that foster competition aimed at making nursing homes a last resort, not a first response for families. Nursing homes are typically viewed as a first response for families because of the current reimbursement system that we have, which encourages families to impoverish their elderly so they can get free nursing home care. The typical situation is this: grandmother lives at home and suffers from dementia. She's not in need of skilled nursing care, she just needs supervision. If she's left alone, she's liable to set the house on fire or wander out in the street and get run over. But mom and dad are a two-parent, wage-earner family and can't stay home. The incentive is to put grandmother in a skilled nursing home facility-the most expensive way to care for her. It is kind of like getting primary care in the emergency room, but that's what Medicaid will pay for. We should be promoting alternatives that foster home- and community-based alternatives: in-home care, adult day care, and respite care services. Imagine if mom and dad could put grandmother in an adult day care center from nine to five. They could pick her up when they come home in the evening,' grandmother stays connected with the

family, the family remains intact, and she avoids the transfer trauma that's incidental to being institutionalized in what she regards as an unfamiliar and hostile facility.
We should foster small group and foster homes for the elderly and we should encourage more nonprofit nursing homes. We need to encourage smaller homes. There's a certain critical mass, a level of occupancy-certainly in the for-profit arena-beyond which you often see a decrement of care. We should consider putting a freeze on building new nursing home beds and channel resources instead to alternative care. As we have promoted institutionalizing the elderly, we have seen a corresponding shrinkage of non-institutional alternatives available to families. Having more options available promotes greater family integrity, keeps families intact and keeps families engaged. The elderly in the family benefit and the youngsters in the family learn something about their social obligation to those who have gone before them.

VOUCHERS, TAX CREDITS OR OTHER INCENTIVES?

What about vouchers, along the lines of the vouchers that we advocate in the educational arena? Why can't we provide families with vouchers that give them the opportunity to shop for alternatives to institutional care? There is a place for skilled nursing facilities on the long-term care continuum, but it should be, as I said earlier, the last resort, not the first response. The taxpayers would save an enormous amount of money by fostering less intensive, less costly alternatives, and the elderly would be greatly advantaged by it.
What about tax credits, tax breaks, or other tax incentives? In Arizona, we have seen the value of educational tax credits and how the credits have promoted alternative forms of education for poor children who wouldn't otherwise have had that ability to go to a school of their own choosing. Why can't we encourage a similar system for the care of our elderly?

What about permitting non-penalized withdrawals from people's IRAs and 401(k)s to encourage taking care of their elderly loved ones? There really is a whole array of options available to us that will have a dramatic impact on the quality of care of our elderly if we'll simply put our thinking caps on, if we'll be alert to the problem and be willing to engage this issue.

The character of a culture is best evidenced by the way in which it treats its frailest, most vulnerable members of society. The current state of affairs in terms of how we treat the elderly in our country does not reflect well on our national character. That's why I am so pleased to join with you in this effort to help build a culture of life in our country-to sound a new call to the restoration of human dignity. Thanks and God bless you.

This publication is adapted from a speech Ken Connor delivered on April 17, 2002, when he was President of Family Research Council. Connor is currently the chairman of the Center for a Just Society based in Washington, DC, and a practicing trial attorney.

ENDNOTES

1 Margery Williams, The Velveteen Rabbit, http://www.writepage.com/velvet.htm.
2 Ibid.

3 Ibid.
4 Wesley J. Smith, Culture of Death: The Assault on Medical Ethics in America (San Francisco: Encounter Books, 2000), p. xiii.
5 Ibid., p. 11.
6 Ibid., p. 12.
7 Federal Interagency Forum on Aging-Related Statistics, Older Americans 2000: Key Indicators of Well-Being, http://www.agingstats.gov/chartbook2000/population.html.
8 Ibid.
9 Richard P. Teske, "Elder Care Politics 101: How Misguided Public Policy Has Created a Crisis," Family Policy (July-August 2001), p. 8.
10 Ibid.
11 Ibid.
12 Nursing Homes: More Can Be Done to Protect Residents from Abuse, GAO-02-312 (Washington, D.C.: March 2002), p. 1.
13 Ibid., p. 4.
14 Ibid.
15 Ibid.
16 Ibid.
17 Ibid.
18 Ibid., p. 8.
19 Ibid.
20 Ibid.
21 Ibid.
22 Ibid.
23 Ibid.
24 Ibid., p. 3.
25 Ibid.
26 Abuse of Residents is a Major Problem in U.S. Nursing Homes, U.S. House Committee on Government Reform Report, July 30, 2001, p. i.
27 Ibid., p. 1. The July 2001 report is accessible online at: http://www.house.gov/reform/min/pdfs/pdf_inves/pdf_nursing_abuse_rep.pdf.
28 Ibid.
29 Ibid., p. ii.
30 Nursing Homes: More Can Be Done to Protect Residents from Abuse, GAO-02-312 (Washington, D.C.: March 2002), p. 4.
31 Ibid., p.5.
32 Appropriateness of Minimum Staffing Ratios in Nursing Homes, HCFA (CMS) Report, August 2000, p. E.S.-6. The HCFA (CMS) report is accessible online at: http://www.hcfa.gov/medicaid/reports/rp700hmp.htm.
33 "Elder Abuse Rampant in Nursing Homes, Experts Say," Long-Term Care Wire, April 10, 2002.
34 Charlene Harrington, Ph.D., RN, et al., "Does Investor Ownership of Nursing Homes Compromise the Quality of Care?" American Journal of Public Health (September 2001), p. 1452.
35 Ibid., p.1454.
36 Ibid., pp. 1453-1454.

37 Ibid., p. 1455.
38 Psalm 8:4, King James Version, http://bible.gospelcom.net.
39 Genesis 1:27, King James Version, says "So God created man in his own image, in the image of God created he him; male and female created he them." http://bible.gospelcom.net.
40 James 1:27, New International Version, International Bible Society, http://bible.gospelcom.net.
41 I Timothy 5:3-4, New International Version, International Bible Society, http://bible.gospelcom.net.
42 New International Version, International Bible Society, http://bible.gospelcom.net.
43 Proverbs 23:22, New International Version, International Bible Society, http://bible.gospelcom.net.

TESTIMONY TO THE HOUSE OF REPRESENTATIVES APRIL 19, 2005

ALTERNATIVES TO LONG TERM CARE FOR THOSE THAT NEED PERSONAL ASSISTANCE TO REMAIN IN THE COMMUNITY

ENDING THE INSTITUTIONAL BIAS IN LONG TERM SERVICES AND SUPPORTS

SUBMITTED IN WRITING BY BOB KAFKA ADAPT

Bob Kafka
ADAPT
1339 LAMAR SQ DR SUITE 101
AUSTIN, TEXAS 78704
512/442-0252
ADAPT@ADAPT.ORG
WWW.ADAPT.ORG

Thank you for the opportunity for to submit written testimony on the issue of community alternatives to long term care and ending the institutional bias in long-term service and support programs.

ADAPT, is the largest grassroots, activist disability rights organization in the country. ADAPT has networks throughout the country. ADAPT works on promoting the rights and services that result in people with disabilities of all ages to live and receive services in the most integrated setting. ADAPT was established in 1979 and is based in Austin, Texas and Denver, Colorado.

Outline of Testimony

I. Statement of Issues
II. Data
III. Legislative Solutions
  A. Short Term
  B. Long Term
IV. Administrative Remedies
V. Issue Areas
  A. Most Integrated Setting
  B. Consumer Direction
  C. Nurse/Physician Delegation/Assignment
  D. Worker/Personnel Issues

STATEMENT OF ISSUES

The number of people with mental and/or physical disabilities and older Americans needing ongoing support services is growing at a rapid rate. The aging of the American population is well documented. The baby boomers are moving into old age. With age comes the higher chance of acquiring some type of physical and/or mental disability. What is not as obvious and is not as well documented is the growing number of children and young adults who also need similar ongoing support services. These numbers are growing due to the advancements in medical technology, rehabilitation techniques and new life saving drugs.

The overwhelming numbers of people with disabilities, old and young, want long-term service and support services in their own homes and communities. The crux of the problem is that these support services currently are provided:

- Mostly in institutionalized setting,
- In an overly medical way that is frequently unnecessary and costly,
- Only when people "spend down" to poverty and get on Medicaid.

The current long term service and support system was originally developed in 1965 when the Medicare and Medicaid programs were created. These funding streams were originally designed and continue to have an institutional bias that favors nursing homes and other institutions over home and community services.
Medicare funds mostly acute care services but not ongoing support services after the acute episode. Medicare Home Health, though community based, was conceived as short-term assistance after a hospital stay but was never designed to provide ongoing long term services and supports for chronic conditions.
Medicaid, the state run federally matched program for low-income people, created an entitlement to nursing home services that states had to provide to all eligible low-income people if the state was to receive any Medicaid funds. Home and community services were then, and remain now, optional services that states may choose to provide. This has resulted in Medicaid becoming the largest funder of institutional long-term service and support programs.

The states are experiencing dramatic budget crises and Medicaid services are a large part of the issue. Because of this institutional bias, States are forced to make dramatic cuts in community services.

People with disabilities, older Americans families, providers, bureaucrats, professionals and politicians all dislike the current system. Reform has defied a political solution. Everyone knows most people want home and community services to be the first priority; however, Congress has not acted to make the public's desire a reality.

DATA

Below are two charts that tell part of the story about the institutional funding bias and the folks in nursing homes today who have expressed an interest in returning to the community.

62% of our long-term care funding comes from public funding. Over $82 billion (1/3rd of all Medicaid funding) is spent on long-term care programs. 70% of this ($57.4 billion) is spent on institutional services, leaving only 30% ($24.7 billion) for ALL home and community services. (See Chart 1)

Chart 2 tells the story that almost 19% of those in nursing homes today want out. This statistic, in all likelihood, is actually low because the question is asked – and data collected -- by a nursing home staff person. But even with these conservative numbers, over 250,000 residents of nursing homes currently want to return home with community services rather than stay in the nursing home. This is a strong argument against the institutional bias and for a money follows the individual program, and for a Real Choice/Community First national policy!

CHART 1

MEDICAID LONG TERM CARE DATA – 2002

(September 2001 through September 2002)

Total Medicaid	*$243.50 billion*	
Total Long Term Care	*82.13 billion*	
	LTC - 33.7% of Medicaid	

##

Nursing Homes	*$ 46.53 billion*	
ICF-MR (public)	*6.47 billion*	
ICF-MR (private)	*4.41 billion*	
Total Institutional	*57.41 billion*	*70%*
Personal Care	*$ 5.55 billion*	
HCBS Waivers	*16.41 billion*	
Home Health	*2.76 billion*	
Total Community	*$ 24.72 billion*	*30%*

##

HCBS WAIVER BREAKDOWN 2002 BY CATEGORY

Total HCBS Waivers	*$ 16.31 billion (adjusted figures)*	*approximate*
MR/DD	*$ 12.03 billion*	*73.8%*
Aged/Disabled	*3.08 billion*	*18.9%*
Physical Disability	*395.25 million*	*2.4%*
Aged	*515.83 million*	*3.2%*
Tech Dependent	*88.82 million*	*.5%*
Brain Injury	*104.73 million*	*.6%*
AIDS/ARC	*66.17 million*	*.4%*
Mental Illness	*32.36 million*	*.2%*

Numbers are taken from a report by MEDSTAT (www.medstat.com) The MEDSTAT Group Inc. – (617)492-9300

MEDSTAT data taken from CMS 64 reports submitted by the states

CHART 2

CMS's December 31, 2003 Minimum Data Set (MDS) Numbers for Question Q1a

Question Q1a - Discharge Potential and Overall Status
Resident Expresses/Indicates Preference to Return to the Community

The way to use the chart below:

Take the State Total number and multiply by the percent that answered Yes -
This will get you the number of people in nursing homes in your state that want to get out of nursing homes and return to the community.

Example:

State: Texas
State Total: 88,072
Percent that answered Yes: 15.5%
Want to Return to the Community: 13,651 people (88,072 X 15.5%)

The number of people who answer yes on the MDS can be the priority population for your State's Olmstead efforts.

The ADAPT Community
www.adapt.org

http://www.cms.hhs.gov/states/mdsreports

Centers for Medicare & Medicaid Services
MDS Active Resident Information Report: December 31, 2003
Q1a: Discharge Potential and Overall Status
Resident Expresses/Indicates Preference to Return to the Community

To view a description of the report table contents, click here.

State	No	Yes	State Total
Alabama	85.9%	14.1%	22,991
Alaska	74.1%	25.9%	607
Arizona	74.6%	25.4%	12,342
Arkansas	84.3%	15.7%	17,937
California	78.2%	21.8%	103,291
Colorado	79.0%	21.0%	15,806
Connecticut	80.4%	19.6%	27,352
Delaware	79.4%	20.6%	3,821
District of Columbia	82.9%	17.1%	2,747
Florida	76.6%	23.4%	69,943
Georgia	86.0%	14.0%	35,327
Hawaii	85.4%	14.6%	3,682
Idaho	75.0%	25.0%	4,570
Illinois	80.6%	19.4%	77,228
Indiana	82.7%	17.3%	39,659
Iowa	82.8%	17.2%	26,835
Kansas	83.4%	16.6%	20,381
Kentucky	83.2%	16.8%	22,088
Louisiana	89.5%	10.5%	28,087
Maine	79.1%	20.9%	6,698
Maryland	77.9%	22.1%	24,664
Massachusetts	82.1%	17.9%	44,393
Michigan	76.9%	23.1%	41,062
Minnesota	80.8%	19.2%	34,515
Mississippi	90.0%	10.0%	15,598
Missouri	80.1%	19.9%	37,301

Montana	78.6%	21.4%	5,565
Nebraska	81.4%	18.6%	13,057
Nevada	78.0%	22.0%	4,091
New Hampshire	84.2%	15.8%	6,957
New Jersey	80.9%	19.1%	43,190
New Mexico	77.3%	22.7%	6,265
New York	81.8%	18.2%	111,244
North Carolina	82.1%	17.9%	37,451
North Dakota	85.7%	14.3%	6,028
Ohio	78.3%	21.7%	76,541
Oklahoma	84.4%	15.6%	20,684
Oregon	73.3%	26.7%	8,165
Pennsylvania	83.6%	16.4%	77,846
Puerto Rico	44.4%	55.6%	169
Rhode Island	83.2%	16.8%	8,345
South Carolina	83.2%	16.8%	15,981
South Dakota	84.9%	15.1%	6,652
Tennessee	81.0%	19.0%	32,697
Texas	84.5%	15.5%	88,072
U.S. Virgin Islands	70.0%	*	30
Utah	70.0%	30.0%	5,187
Vermont	79.3%	20.7%	3,208
Virginia	78.9%	21.1%	27,444
Washington	74.7%	25.3%	19,410
West Virginia	78.6%	21.4%	10,129
Wisconsin	80.1%	19.9%	35,134
Wyoming	78.0%	22.0%	2,415
NATIONAL TOTAL	81.1%	18.9%	1,410,882

** Less than 10 responses.*

Table counts exclude missing responses or responses in cells with 10 or less responses. A cell entry of "<0.05%" indicates that there were at least 11 responses for the column value.
Source: MDS National Repository

Select different report | Select different date

LEGISLATIVE SOLUTONS

Short Term Solutions

The Administration has proposed a bill known as the "New Freedom Initiative Medicaid Demonstration Act". This includes a section on Money Follows the Individual: in this concept, any individual who chooses to leave the nursing home or other institution could have the funds being spent on their institutional services moved to cover the cost of their services in the community. Senator(s) Smith and Harkin have introduced a bill which is a stand alone Money Follows the Individual bill. ADAPT strongly supports Money Following the Person and demonstration programs to encourage states to follow such a policy. ADAPT believes one or both of these bills must be passed this session.

Another action Congress can take, as an incentive for states to choose home and community services, would be to increase the FMAP by 5%-10% when a state chooses home and community services. This would leave the nursing home entitlement as is, but give states an economic incentive to choose home and community services.

Long Term Solutions

MiCASSA, the Medicaid Community Attendant Services and Supports Act, S 971, would allow real choice, money follow the person and enhance consumer direction. Simply, if you are eligible for a nursing home or ICF-MR facility you can choose instead to have a community service titled "Community Attendant Services and Supports". You could select to have this service delivered through the traditional agency model, fiscal intermediary, or voucher system. MiCASSA would assure that no one goes into a nursing home or other institution because of lack of options, and it would assure greater consumer control of services. It assures REAL CHOICE.

The bigger fix would be to reform the entire system and separate out health care funding from long term services and supports. This requires developing a social model of long term services and supports that is coordinated but not linked to the acute/health system . This reform would include in one system those with physical and/or mental disabilities, older Americans and children with disabilities with low/middle/high incomes who need Activities of Daily Living (ADL) and/or Independent Activities of Daily Living (IADL) assistance, as well as cognitive supports.

This bigger fix would require developing a "Long Term Services and Supports, LTSS, Fund" that would include the current dollars in the

Medicare/Medicaid used for long term services and supports, as well as a new funding source to meet the growing needs of the US population.

ADAPT is opposed to any block grant proposals that would arbitrarily cap dollars and force reduction in services and numbers of people on programs.

ADMINISTRATIVE REMEDIES

The Center for Medicaid and Medicare Services, CMS, could do many things to end the institutional bias through changes in rules and policies to enhances community services. These include:

- **Put consumer direction in ALL community programs**
- **Relax any requirements for the person to be homebound or unnecessary medical requirements**
- **Ease restrictions on how states can use Minimum Data Set, MDS, data**
- **Add a requirement that federally authorized entities such as Centers for Independent Living and Area Agencies on Aging be involved when a nursing home resident in chooses to live in the community.**
- **Require a "most integrated setting" question as part of the process of getting into a nursing home or other institution**
- **Create incentives for discharge planners at hospitals and rehabilitation facilities to promote community placements.**

Congress should work with CMS to encourage administrative fixes.

ISSUE AREAS

A. Most Integrated Setting/Olmstead

States still have not adequately complied with the Supreme Court's 1996 Olmstead decision which said that unnecessary institutionalization of people with disabilities is discrimination. Congress should put language in the US Dept. of Health and Human Services, HHS, budget bill directing HHS to monitor and ensure states are getting and keeping folks out of nursing homes and other institutions. Dept of Justice and HHS/Office of Civil Rights, OCR, should be directed to assure no civil rights abuses are taking place by folks not getting/staying out of nursing homes and other institutions.

B. Consumer Direction

A consumer directed philosophy should permeate any and all Congressional legislation. This is not an agency – consumer directed dichotomy; in other words agency provided services can be consumer directed as well as voucher

type services. We would be happy to provide more information on this if asked.

ADAPT Definition of Consumer Direction

As it relates to program design for attendant services, consumer direction means the right of the consumer to select, manage and dismiss an attendant.

The consumer has this right regardless of who serves as the employer of record, and whether or not that individual needs assistance directing his or her services.

This includes but not limited to delivery systems that use:

Vouchers
Direct cash
Fiscal intermediaries
Agencies that allow choice (Agencies with Choice)
Concept included in MiCASSA

C. Nurse/Physician Delegation/Assignment

One of the most costly aspects of community programs is the over medicalization of services. ADAPT is for quality of services, but we know quality can be accomplished without unnecessary medical involvement. Delegation/ Assignment of tasks is working in states across the country. Though Congress may not be able to address the issue directly, you could make recommendations and develop incentives for states to work with advocates to provide "quality services" without unnecessary medical intrusion.

D. Worker/Personnel Issues

The shortage of well paid home care workers is reaching epidemic proportions. Some of it is the low wages and no benefits of the occupation. Congress needs to develop incentives to bring together consumers, family members, providers, attendants, administrators and union representatives to develop recommendations on how to enhance the pool of workers available to do home care services.

Bob Kafka
ADAPT
1339 LAMAR SQ DRIVE SUITE 101
AUSTIN, TEXAS 78704

512/442-0252 **512/431-4085 CELL** **BKAFKA@JUNO.COM**

Testimony Before the Subcommittee on
Criminal Justice, Drug Policy and Human Resources
Of the Committee on Government Reform
Of the U.S. House of Representatives

Oversight Hearing on
"Federal Health Programs and
Those Who Cannot Care for Themselves:
What Are Their Rights,
And Our Responsibilities?"

April 19, 2005

Arthur Caplan PhD
Chair
Department of Medical Ethics
and
Director, Center for Bioethics
University of Pennsylvania

I very much appreciate the opportunity to provide testimony to the Subcommittee. I am going to focus my testimony on three key themes; (1) what needs to be done to adequately protect the rights and interests of those Americans who cannot care for themselves?, (2) what did the Terri Schiavo case teach us about the adequacy of existing mechanisms for protecting those who are in a PVS state or severely cognitively disabled and what protections exist for those who are incapacitated to ensure that their constitutional rights of due process are met?, (3) whether the various legal instruments used to express the wishes of the incapacitated are sufficient to guide their care?

What, if anything, needs to be done to fix existing protections for those who cannot care for themselves?

The question, coming as it does in the wake of the Schiavo case, both as it was battled out in the state of Florida and in the Federal Courts as well as Congress, presumes that something in the existing system of legal protections for those who are unable to communicate their wishes about medical treatment and technologies is broken. There are those testifying before this Sub-committee who argue that the system is broken and worse that there are those who do not want to treat Americans with severe disabilities and impairments either because they are biased against those with disabilities or because they seek to save money by rushing such persons off to an early grave. I think these arguments are deeply flawed.

Let me simply state there there is no evidence, none, that any health care institution is seeking to end the lives of any American for reasons of cost. I do not think there is any effort underway for example to limit or stop care for the thousands of Americans who are now in PVS states or severely brain damaged states in our nursing homes or hospitals. Contrary to what was often suggested in the discussion of the Terri Schiavo case saving money or saving society the cost of her care had nothing, absolutely nothing, to do with the reasons her feeding tube was removed. The current protections in place for persons such as Terri would not allow such a reason to motivate such behavior. The reason her feeding tube was stopped was out of consideration for her choices, her values and her wishes and no other reason.

To understand what the protections are for those who cannot speak for themselves we need to distinguish between those who cannot speak for themselves because they have never had the capacity to do so—children and those born with severe and irreversible cognitive deficiencies from birth and those who once were capable of self-determination and voluntary, informed choice but who can no longer speak for themselves. It is the latter category that drew so much attention in the recent national debate about the case of Terri Schiavo. And it that category that my testimony will focus on since for this group liberty and privacy are the values that Congress, constitutionally, must protect.

I do not believe that the system of protections in place for those who once could but can no longer as a result of illness or injury speak for themselves in our health care system is seriously broken or malfunctioning. There is a system in place and, despite all the attention that the case of Terri Schiavo generated suggesting otherwise, the system has worked well and continues to work well in insuring that the rights of those to have or not have medical treatment consistent with their personal values and choices are respected.

What is that system? It is a system of protections that has been in place since the time when Karen Ann Quinlan became the object of a national debate about ending medical treatment for a person unable to speak in 1976. It is a system that many seem to have forgotten exists during the debate about Terri Schiavo. It is a system that Congress ought to both understand and respect. It is a system of protections that needs to be treated with great care and consideration if more harm then good is to be avoided by those who would meddle with it. It is a system that relies on two foundational values—the right to liberty and privacy. And one key procedural protection exists--that families or those close to us can best speak for us if we cannot speak for ourselves about our medical care.

The Protections of Liberty and Privacy

The most important protection that each of us has in this country when it comes to medical care is that it is our individual decision as to what we do or do not want to accept. No one has the right to force us to be a patient. No one has the right to compel any form of intervention upon our bodies be it a pill, a feeding tube, a cold compress, a blood transfusion, a nicotine patch or any other form of medical care and treatment if I, as a competent person who is informed about my options, say 'no'. The adult Jehovah's Witness can refuse a blood transfusion even it means certain death and leaving behind children, family and friends. The Christian Scientist or other believer in the healing power of the divinity may pray instead of entering a hospital. The adult person who does not believe in Western medicine may forgo it. The person who does not want to undergo one more round of chemotherapy or another organ transplant may say enough. And the person who says I do not choose to live a quality of life that can only be maintained by medical means can say no even if their death will inevitably follow that refusal.

Nor do we lose that right when we cannot communicate. The optimal means of securing this right is to either write down our wishes or to designate someone to choose for us. But, many people do not do either of these things often because they cannot afford a lawyer, do not want to think in advance about topics that frighten them, worry that they may actually bring about their death if they write about such things or, as in the case of young people such as Terri Schiavo, Nancy Cruzan, or Karen Ann Quinlan, simply do not see writing out directives about their death as a pressing concern. They still have the right to control their care.

This need to protect liberty and privacy when it comes to medical care triggers the procedural protection long in place for those who can no longer speak for themselves. Their family or those they have lived with most intimately can exercise their autonomy for them.

Family members can express the values and wishes of their loved ones about medical care. Those who know a person best can say what that person would have wanted either on the basis of conversations and discussions or by substituting their judgment about what their loved one would have wanted knowing their core values and beliefs about medicine and about life.

Let me stress that the core value that protects each one of us is that no one has the right to make anyone of us do anything that we do not choose to do. This is a fundamental liberty right. It is also a fundamental privacy right. There are no more important values in guiding the relationships that medicine and government should have toward each American then guaranteeing their right to control what third parties may do to them even in the name of beneficence and the desire to do good.

This means that it would be wrong and indeed unconstitutional to create any presumption in favor of medical care or treatment for a once competent person who can no longer communicate. What must be created is a legal system that listens carefully and intently to try and discern what a person unable to communicate would say about their wishes and choices. Only if no such information can be discerned would any presumption make any sense and even then Congress would have to act with great care in trying to decide what can be presumed about medical care for every American given the range of values and views that exist in this area.

Again the key protection of individual rights that this Sub-committee must concern itself with is not what Congress thinks is best for each person when it comes to health care nor what any particular religious groups think, or disability groups think, or disease advocacy groups, or what any other organized interest group thinks. What matters and what only matters is what the individual thinks. What Congress must do is everything it can to insure that individual liberty and privacy are protected even if a person becomes incapacitated, severely cognitively disabled or otherwise unable to communicate. Those who once had the ability to be autonomous, to be self-determining should not lose that right due to incapacity as state and Federal courts have averred again and again and again since the New Jersey Supreme Court ruled in Quinlan.

Turning to Families and Friends in the Face of Lost Capacity

The place to turn should a person be unable to speak or communicate is to those closest to them. Families should have the authority to decide how best to respect the autonomy and self-determination and the liberty interest of the once competent but now cognitively incapacitated. And when families do not agree then it should be husbands and wives, or those who are de facto in such a role, who should have priority of decision-making authority to act as surrogate decision-makers. Then adult children should have authority. Then parents and other relatives have surrogate authority.

This is the exact line of authority that is used in organ and tissue donation under the Uniform Anatomical Gift Act. It is used for the ethical reason that spouses and adult children are presumed to know best the wishes and values and desires of their family members. In medicine generally, whether it is in the emergency room or in the ICU health care providers turn to spouses first to gain guidance about what a person would have wanted in the way of medical care.

The privileging of spouses makes both ethical and public policy sense. These are the people whom those who can no longer communicate chose to be with. They are the people who are most likely to have heard their most recent expressions of values and choices. They are the persons most likely to be most familiar with the choices and values that the person held at the time they lost the ability to communicate.

Obviously a spouse or adult child or parent can be dismissed from the role of surrogate decision-maker. But the burden of proof must fall on those who would so displace them. And the evidence needed to do so must be compelling lest society show too little regard for the role of husband or wife.

There is no role for strangers and third parties to try and act as surrogates when families are present. There is no role for Congress or any other institutional third party to try and insert itself into the substantive decision-making process. There is a role for the courts but I would argue that role is best served at the local and state court levels where courts have experience with both local values and family disputes. If polls in the wake of the death of Terri Schiavo are to be believed, the American people overwhelming agree that spouses, families and local courts ought be the place to turn to resolve issues concerning the medical care of those once competent but now unable to communicate.

Lessons From Schiavo about adequacy of Procedural Protections

The core system for protecting individual self-determination when the question is starting, stopping, or forgoing medical care relies on liberty and privacy. These values are deemed to be best protected by family members. And within families it is spouses and then adult children who are seen as best suited to protect the liberty and privacy of their loved ones.

But, there is more of a procedural system in place to protect those who once where competent but who can no longer speak for themselves then this. Over the past thirty years we have seen an amazing and prudent system of procedural protection evolve. Some of these procedural protections were in evidence in the Terri Schiavo case. Others were harder to see but they are nonetheless present and functioning well.

Doctors, nurses and health care ethics.

Every person who is very ill in a hospital will have decisions made for him or her about their care. It is not possible nor is it practical to involve the patient or the family in all of these decisions. Some involve what sorts of equipment will be used. Others involve what is available to eat or who it is that will care for you. The protection that patients have, both competent and incompetent, in these areas involved both legal duties of health care workers and institutions as well as professional ethics.

I want to focus on professional ethics since these may be the hardest to observe but they are crucial. Having competent persons assess a patient's status, having hands-on information about a patient's prognosis and optimal care and knowing what the limits are of medical intervention are all crucial to protecting the interests and rights of patients.

Every one of us, if we die in a hospital or nursing home, will have a decision made not to do something for us. There are those, some who are testifying before you today, who would suggest that physicians, hospitals and nursing homes should make no decisions about when to forgo or stop medical care. This is simply nonsense.

Decisions about when to stop CPR, when to abandon efforts to try and continue care on a person with a massive head injury, decisions about whether an operation can be undertaken or not must involve decisions by doctors. Ending resuscitation efforts, to take one example, is not something that anyone except a doctor can decide. A patient or a family might request that everything possible be done but it is the doctor and the hospital that determines possibility not the patient or the family. That is why medical ethics are so very important as a procedural safeguard for patients. That is why the growing trend toward discussing ethics as a key part of the training of doctors and nurses and health care workers is so very important and something that Congress must both encourage and fund.

One other professional ethics protection the vulnerable have is the ethics of institutions. In this regard it is important to state how ethical the institution of hospice is in this country with its commitment to help the terminally ill in an ethical manner. I deeply regret the allegations that were made in the heat of the Schiavo case by those who disagreed with the decision to remove her feeding tube that impugned the ethics of the hospice where she died. I defy critics of hospice or any member of Congress to demonstrate an instance where a hospice has let someone die who is suffering or in pain. Hospice is one of the greatest achievements of American health care. It should not be disparaged. It ought to be allowed to grow and flourish in any way that Congress can.

Ethics Committees

Little was said in the Schiavo case about ethics committees. But since the days of Karen Ann Quinlan hospitals and most nursing homes and hospices have formed such committees. They often deal with end of life care issues and with the rare family dispute when these occur. I think these are very valuable resources to have available but they are not resources that hospitals or nursing homes have chosen to supply with adequate support, education and training. Congress may want to encourage that this situation change.

<u>State Courts</u>

Perhaps the most visible system of protection on display in the Schiavo case was the state court system. In the case of Terri Schiavo long before the involvement by Congress the state courts of Florida had carefully and systematically reviewed the evidence, claims and opinions provided to them by the disputing family members. In my view the state courts of Florida did a superb job of adjudicating a very difficult family dispute. I saw no reason then and still see no reason now to presume that a Federal court or Congress could improve upon the performance of the Florida state courts in the Schiavo case or for that matter in any other case. Local courts and state courts have acquitted themselves with distinction in adjudicating thoughtfully and wisely the very few and exceedingly rare cases that come before them where parties could not agree on a proper course of medical care. These courts have in many instances received guidance from their state legislatures on how to handle various matters involving medical care for the competent and once competent patient. There is absolutely no evidence that this system is broken or in need of any intervention by Congress. There is some reason to believe that any attempt to do so would create far more harm then good.

Are existing legal instruments used to express the wishes of the incapacitated sufficient?

Unfortunately little is known about the use of living wills, advance directives and durable powers of attorney in the United States. Little systematic information exists on how many Americans have such documents. Even less exists on how often they update them.

There is much evidence to suggest, unfortunately, that these documents do not prove useful in clinical settings. Often health care providers do not know them since family members are not aware of their existence. They do not travel well from nursing home to hospital or from hospital to home care. They are often written in a manner that is too vague to be useful as when a person designates their 'family' to make decisions rather than a particular person leaving it unclear who they really meant to act as their surrogate. And sometimes the evidence shows doctors simply ignore the documents more often than not continuing care even when a signed directive requests that this not be done!

There is work to be done in this area to improve these legal instruments. Having a computerized registry would be useful. Allowing people to make up durable power of attorneys and advance directives without having to pay lawyers fees might be helpful. Making sure that every person is given a real chance to fill out such a document in an informed manner upon entry to a hospital or nursing home as well as upon entry to the military or even when registering to vote might help.

However, many persons are simply not going to fill these documents out. This should not be the basis for making any presumption about what the person might have wanted. In lieu of such a document it is still best, in my view, to turn to the closest family member or in the absence of family member, closest knowledgeable friend and let them try to articulate the values and choices the once competent but now incapacitated person would have made. Does this approach mean error is possible? It does. However, far more risk of error exists when the law presumes that only one answer is possible or that complete strangers can make the best decisions for those who cannot communicate.